"Gone with the Wind," He Said

"Gone with the Wind," He Said

The Cold Case Search for My
Missing-in-Action Airman Brother

Michael I. Darter

Library of Congress Control Number:		2014900686
ISBN:	Hardcover	978-1-4931-6253-6
	Softcover	978-1-4931-6252-9
	eBook	978-1-4931-6254-3

Rev. date: 02/03/2014

To order additional copies of this book, contact:
Xlibris LLC
1-888-795-4274
www.Xlibris.com
Orders@Xlibris.com
543034

CONTENTS

PERSPECTIVE

"During the summer of 1943 a fierce battle raged in the skies over Europe. Every day, hundreds of young airmen faced death as they flew bombing raids deep into enemy territory. Fewer and fewer were coming back." (*Memphis Belle*, motion picture, Warner Bros., 1990)

"Of all the combat jobs in the American services during World War II, from infantryman to submariner, no job was more dangerous, statistically, than that of a man in a bomber over Germany. The Eighth and Fifteenth Air Forces took a higher percentage of losses than any other American fighting force, from foxhole to destroyer deck.

"Nevertheless, in spite of severe testing of even the highest morale, *particularly during the summer and fall of 1943*, American bomber crews did their jobs day after day, going up against the roughest flak and fighter defenses ever conceived. Because prewar planners believed bombers could get through without fighter protection had a great deal to do with the number of American losses." (Jeffrey L. Ethel, *Bomber Command*, ISBN 0-87938-920-6, published by Motorbooks International Publishers & Wholesalers, 1994)

POW/MIA Flag

PREFACE

My older brother S/Sgt. Eugene F. Darter became missing on his first US Army Air Corps bombing mission over Germany on December 16, 1943. He was not reported to be in any POW camps, did not return home after the war ended, and was assumed to be killed in action by the government. Our parents, however, refused to accept that he had died and strongly believed he would someday return home. There was always this continuing feeling of uncertainty in our home, and there was never any end to the grieving and wondering what happened and why he had not returned home. Of course there was no closure.

After our parents died, I had a memorial headstone placed next to our father's grave, which I visited often, clutching his Purple Heart, and thought about him over the years, constantly wondering about what happened on the mission he was lost on and how and where he died and of course wondering if his remains could be discovered and brought home and given the honor he deserved. I never imagined that this "cold case" could be solved.

Then late one evening, on his January 3, 2000, birthday, just over fifty-seven years after he vanished, I instinctively typed B-17 into Yahoo! Search. What I learned that night set me on a long and challenging journey to determine what happened to my only brother. I soon became painfully aware of the huge number of MIAs that still exist from World War II and also from all other wars and the pain that so many families experience over this uncertainty for so many years. This book tells the true story of my search and the mind-boggling discoveries and miracles that occurred until closure was finally achieved on a Dutch island in the North Sea.

This very cold case appeared to be hopeless in the beginning, but through modern Internet search techniques, government and other databases, the National Archives records, and Google Earth, my family and friends were amazingly able to discover through eyewitnesses what happened to my only brother and his crewmates on their fateful combat mission over Nazi Germany. I strongly encourage other families who have MIAs to conduct their search. Because today there are so many helpful tools and databases and records that are available, along with very helpful assistance from the US Joint POW/MIA Accounting Command (JPAC) and the Defense POW/Missing Personnel Office (DPMO) whose motto is "Keeping the Promise" to bring our MIAs home. There are also privately funded, nonprofit organizations that are very effective in locating MIAs for JPAC to bring home.

I have had the great blessings to help raise five wonderful children and to experience a long and fulfilling civil engineering and academic career. However, this journey over more than a decade to find my only brother has been even more satisfying and rewarding. So I urge anyone who has an MIA in their family to begin the journey to find as much as you can about his or her life and sacrifice. Chances are you will be successful at some level, given all the information and assistance available today.

This book tells the story of the search for my American airman brother (he is also my children's uncle and my grandchildren's great-uncle) and his crewmates who served in the Army Air Force in World War II in the most dangerous theater: the bloody skies of Nazi-occupied Europe. Over twenty-six thousand American airmen gave their lives over Europe, more than the entire Marine Corps in WWII. Over seven thousand airmen became and are still MIA. The X-files of these MIAs show their bravery in paying the ultimate sacrifice for our freedom. And yes, I'm very proud to know that my brother and his brave B-17 crewmates were part of the great effort that stopped the murderous Nazis by destroying their military and industrial facilities and thereby helped to control the air so that Allied soldiers could land on the beach on D-Day.

ACKNOWLEDGMENTS

So many people and organizations helped me on this long journey to discover what happened to my MIA brother and his crew in World War II. I am so grateful to the 95th Bomb Group Memorial Associations in the United States and in the United Kingdom for their encouragement and assistance over the last thirteen years. At the annual reunions of the 95th, I met several veterans, Art Watson, Robert Cousins, Ed Charles, Russ Brainhart, John Story, John Miller, Eugene Fletcher, John Walter, and many more, who provided me with invaluable information about their experiences at Horham. In fact, John Miller and Eugene Fletcher flew their B-17F, the *Lonesome Polecat II*, and Art Watson knew the Flying Fortress well and described its nose art and where it parked on the base.

A huge thank-you to the surviving crew members, including Charlie Schreiner, for his detailed letter written to pilot Lt. Fred Delbern's wife, Geri; Doral Hupp (and son Rod Hupp), for his account of saving my brother's life on the plane; Loren Dodson, who was my brother's best friend and who gave me so much insight about him; and Pete Jackson, for his account of the mission. These were all eyewitness accounts. Much gratitude to my University of Texas classmate John Woollen, son of crewmate Ed Woollen, for sharing his father's experience and providing his beautiful memorial written to his three fallen crewmates. Thanks to Rosemary McKeegan, wife of Bob McKeegan, for all the information about her husband.

Extra big thanks to Geri Marshall (Delbern), for her insights about the crew members, especially her amazing first husband, pilot Fred Delbern. Thanks to the nephews of Geri Marshall, Dane Hanson and Charlie Hanson, for discovering my first book on the crew, their search and discovery of the copilot's wife. Recently, a niece of Fred Delbern, Gayle Gondek, was located in Minnesota; and we were able to share the discoveries with her and her family. Thanks to the sons of Marjorie Stanley, wife of copilot Don Neff. Brian and Bruce Burk are the sons of Marjorie's second husband, whom she married after the war. They were very kind to provide information on their mother and her first wedding photo with Don Neff.

Thanks to Johan Graas and his North Holland World War II Aircraft Recovery Association, for his untiring and tremendous help in locating information on Texel Island and speaking at the memorials in May 2007 and June 2013. This man and his friends deserve so much for their lifelong efforts to recover many American and UK flight crews who became MIAs in Holland.

Thanks to numerous individuals who live near the old 95th Horham airbase, including Frank and Jane Sherman, Alan Johnson, James Mutton, Norman Feltwell, and many more. These men and women have restored the Red Feather Club with their blood, sweat, and tears over the past thirteen years to beyond anything imaginable and to the great delight of the veterans, who now in their late eighties and nineties still return to Horham to renew their friendships.

And of course there are no words to express my gratitude to Cornelius Ellen from Texel for sharing his heartbreaking experience in seeing the last moments of my brother's life out in the stormy and freezing Wadden Sea. Over the past ten years, Cornelius showed great kindness and participated in many interviews and walks into the Wadden Sea to search for Eugene.

Cornelius's eyewitness account of the American airman splashing down in the Wadden Sea and then was pulled by his parachute and was "gone with the wind" helped greatly to bring closure to the family. And also so much gratitude to his son John, daughter-in-law Naomi, and grandson Alexander for all of their friendship and help, year after year, in so many ways on Texel.

On Texel Island, thanks to the Betsema brothers (Gerrit and Jack) whose father saw the Polecat over their Oost village and who provided a boat for holding a memorial on the Wadden Sea and searching for the sunken aircraft in the North Sea. The special prepared by TV North Holland was helpful in getting the word out. Mr. Gerard Timmerman of the Texelse Courant published several articles about my visits that led to the discovery of eyewitnesses including Mr. Cees Bonnie and Mr.

Michele Binsbergen who were children in De Koog when the terrifying roar of the B-17 came just over their roof tops. Mr. P. K. Stark told how he met two of the crewmembers after they were captured by German soldiers. Mr. Jaap Bakker located the diary of Mr. K. Kok who heard the crash of the B-17 in the North Sea.

Thank you to Paul Dekker from Texel, who located pieces of the *Polecat* (B17) on the beach and turned them in to the museum on Texel in May 2007, thereby participating in a miracle. Paul has continued to give our family pieces of the B-17 that are found each year with his metal detector. Thank you to Bram van Dijk and Jan Nieuwenhuis of Texel WW II museum for his help in the search, the WW II display at the museum, and the luncheon with the eyewitnesses. Much gratitude to Hans Eelman for his assistance with the search for the "unknowns" in the Wadden Sea area. At great personal expense, Hans conducted a sonar survey of the General area of beach marker Paal 19 near De Koog, Texel, with his fishing boat in August 2012, where four eyewitnesses heard or observed the crash and the fishing boats lost their nets in the 1980s.

Appreciation is expressed to the National Archives II located in Silver Spring, Maryland, for maintaining so much information, as without these documents, much would not be known. Huge thanks is also expressed to several units of the Department of Defense: the Defense POW/Missing Personnel Office (DPMO) conducted a recent up-to-date investigation on my brother using all of the available records; and the Freedom of Information and Privacy Act Office, Army Human Resources Command's Freedom of Information Act program (502) 613-4203, who provided me with all the X-files of Unknowns from the American Cemetery at Margraten, Netherlands.

Finally, so much appreciation is expressed to my five children (Michelle, Michael, Paul, Sonya, and Rebecca), their spouses (Terrin, Dana, and Lynn), and three grandchildren (Alex, Lorren, and Ava) and Vivien Prince for their patience and help in the investigation on Texel and in the search for Eugene in the Wadden Sea and in the many discussions on what happened during the mission and in reviewing this manuscript.

Oh yes, and thanks to whoever provided that "message from beyond" (piece of the B-17) on the North Sea beach to our family and all the families of the crew members of the Lonesome Polecat II *on May 4, 2007.*

CHAPTER 1

VANISHED

Meeting My Brother

It was late, and the January 3, 2000, winter night was cold as I began preparing to head home from my University of Illinois office. As I scanned my calendar, I suddenly realized that today was my older brother Eugene's birthday. He would have been eighty-seven years old on this day had he not vanished in the skies over Nazi Europe. Without consciously trying, somehow my fingers typed B-17 into Yahoo! Search, and I hit the Enter key. Up came several Web sites of American units that flew from England. I opened one and read some tearful stories of family members searching for their fathers, grandfathers, uncles, and even brothers who had become missing in action (MIA) during the air war over Europe in World War II. I opened another and then another unit Web site and found the same thing. Over an hour passed quickly. I thought, my god, those are the helpless feelings of missing a loved one that my family has felt for more than fifty years for my MIA brother Eugene. Ever since I can remember, the question of what happened to my only brother has been a *big* family struggle. Where did he die? How did he die? Or did he die?

My parents told me about my older brother Eugene many times as I was growing up. He was a smart kid (with a photographic memory, his best friend told me later) and a very hardworking boy, but also a young man who loved to play practical jokes. Born in Long Beach, California, on January 3, 1913, he graduated from Long Beach Polytechnic High

School, which is a distinguished school in both academics and athletics. More University of California admissions come from this high school than any other in California, and *Sports Illustrated* magazine named Polytechnic the Sports School of the Century in 2005, and he loved and participated in various sports.

Eugene F. Darter at the Long Beach Polytechnic High School graduation
(Photo credit M. I. Darter)

Eugene went on to attend college for four years, working all the time at a drug store, and also started his own security business. He was very patriotic courageous too as I read some of his old personal letters and I saw references that he had served as an undercover agent for the United States government to investigate Communist activity in the LA area and had done very well at it with some strong recommendations. I discovered that at twenty-nine years of age, he enlisted in the US Army on October 30, 1942, in Los Angeles. He volunteered for the US Army Air Corps and passed all of the rigorous requirements and began extensive training over the next year and became a radio operator and gunner crew member on a B-17 bomber.

I visited Long Beach several times when growing up, met my sister Hazel and Eugene's mother Estella (we had the same father Frank Darter but different mothers), and got sunburned on that beautiful "long beach" every time. But most important, and maybe this describes my lifelong bonding to him, my parents told me that I actually met Eugene during his last furlough home on leave in August 1943, just before departure for war. They told me that he was so thrilled to meet his two-month-old baby brother but nervous about carrying such a tiny creature around that he asked for a pillow and placed me lovingly on it. He then carried me all around the neighborhood, showing me to everyone he met. But soon, he had to leave to meet his crew and his destiny in the worldwide bloody war that was upon us. I'm told that Dad and mother, Eugene, and I (in his arms) held hands and prayed on our knees for his safe return. And then he departed and vanished from our lives forever, except in our hearts.

S/Sgt. Eugene F. Darter, 1943 (Photo credit M. I. Darter)

The raging air war news from Europe in the fall of 1943 was not good and made our parents very nervous. Day after day, terribly fierce aerial battles were under way, and hundreds of young Americans in bombers and fighters were being killed, as were our enemies. We were fighting the German Luftwaffe, the largest and most technologically advanced modern air force in the world, and we were sending our bombers over industrial targets deeper and deeper into Europe in broad daylight. Newspapers reported on the disastrous consequences and controversy of American bombers filled with some of our best young men having little fighter protection in the summer and fall of 1943 over Nazi Europe being slaughtered every day. On October 14, 1943, there was a mission to Schweinfurt, Germany, that made newspaper headlines, where sixty US heavy bombers carrying six hundred crew members were shot down. These massive losses were of grave concern to the families and the many airmen preparing to ship out.

The last letter from Eugene was for Dad's November 27 birthday from "somewhere in England" filled with both fear and optimism and of course love for his family. Just four weeks thereafter, however, a telegram was received at our home from the War Department that S/Sgt. Eugene F. Darter had been shot down and become missing on a mission over Germany on December 16, 1943. My parents and Eugene's mother and my sister were devastated. As time went on, there was still no report of him being a prisoner of war (POW) either. Thus, he became officially killed in action (KIA) and was still missing in action (MIA). But definitely he was still alive, I was told by my parents and Eugene's mother as I was growing up for years afterward.

What Happened to My Brother?

Several years later, when I was in high school, my father gave me a very old yellowed letter from the US Army Air Corps dated just after he was shot down. It said that Eugene was a crew member on a B-17 bomber on a mission to Bremen, Germany, when his plane was hit by flak going into the bomb run. The Flying Fortress dropped out of formation and was then attacked by several enemy fighters. Three chutes were reported coming out of the stricken bomber, which was last seen twenty-nine miles west of Bremen entering into clouds.

Aircraft B-17F, #42-30255 departed on a mission to Bremen, Germany, 16 December 1943. The aircraft is thought to have been hit by anti-aircraft fire just before reaching the target. The #3 engine was lost causing the plane to drop back out of formation. It continued over the target, dropped its bombs, losing altitude and dropping further behind the formation. Fighters were then seen

to attack the B-17 and three chutes were reported. The aircraft
continued losing altitude but seemed otherwise under control until
it disappeared in the clouds about 53° 05' N and 08° 05' E.

Well, the war ended in May 1945, the POWs returned home, but Eugene did not. Our parents wrote repeated letters to the government, asking for more information. A few letters were received from the government a few years after the war, but nothing of substance was ever relayed. Ironically, our parents never believed that he had died. They constantly told me that he was likely wounded, became a German prisoner, escaped, and waited out the war in the Soviet-occupied territory. Perhaps he mentioned how much he disdained communism and ended up in a Soviet prison. But, they said, Eugene would get out someday and return home. Parents' love often trumps reality. They refused to even have a memorial headstone placed years later, but I did so immediately after their death, as this was an ongoing traumatic discussion in our home for decades.

Tomb of the Unknown, Could This Be Him?

In 1969, I traveled to Washington DC for the first time and visited the Tomb of the Unknowns in Arlington National Cemetery. As I watched the ceremony of Changing the Guard, I was so moved that chills went through my entire body, tears went down my face, and I began wondering if the World War II unknown could be my brother.

I learned that the Tomb of the Unknowns was first created when the World War I unknown chosen from four identical caskets in France was interred in 1921. The selection and the interment of the World War II unknown occurred in 1958. Each unknown was selected from remains exhumed from cemeteries in Europe, Africa, Hawaii, and the Philippines. The procedure of selection was one unknown from the European/African areas and one from the Pacific area were placed in identical caskets and taken aboard a navy ship. Then Navy First Class William R. Charette, then the US Navy's only active-duty Medal of Honor recipient, selected the World War II unknown. The remaining casket received a burial at sea.

The caskets from World War II and the Korean War arrived in Washington on May 28, 1958, where they lay in the Capitol Rotunda until the morning of May 30, when they were carried on caissons to

Arlington National Cemetery. President Eisenhower awarded each the Medal of Honor, and the unknowns of World War II and the Korean War were interred beside their World War I comrade.

This process was obviously designed so that anyone who has a beloved family member who is missing in action (MIA) would think that it is possible that the unknown from any one of these wars is their loved one. It sure worked for me because my MIA brother, S/Sgt Eugene Francis Darter of the US Army Air Corps, was lost somewhere west of Bremen, Germany and could have been buried somewhere in the heart of Europe with no identification on his remains.

Just How Many MIAs Are There?

Here is a summary of the number of unknowns from World War II onward, current to December 4, 2012.[44, 45]

- World War II: 73,677
- Korean War: 7,938
- Vietnam War: 1,655
- Cold War: 126
- Iraq and other conflicts: 6
- Operation Enduring Freedom (Afghanistan War): 1

This means 83,403 families are still waiting to learn what happened to their beloved son, daughter, brother, sister, uncle, aunt, father, mother, or grandparents. These numbers simply stagger the imagination. But as I also discovered, the United States has for decades spent many millions of dollars every single year to search for our MIA unknowns and return their remains to their families. Why? The consistent promise to our servicemen and servicewomen is that "we will never leave you behind. We will bring you home no matter what it takes because that is our promise to you and your families deserve an answer." Who could argue with this attitude? Certainly not any of the thousands of families still waiting for an answer.

Left: Tomb of the Unknowns in Arlington National Cemetery
(Photo credit M. I. Darter)

Right: POW-MIA flag placed in US Capitol Rotunda to remain
"until they all return" (Photo credit M. I. Darter)

Government and Other Help in the Search for MIAs

The US government has long been involved in trying to identify and bring home its MIA service members. The *Quartermaster Review* on its May/June 1946 issue reported on the Graves Registration search and recovery operations at the end of World War II,

> *The most intensive search in history is being conducted on the far-flung battlefields of World War II. Identification and proper burial of unknown American servicemen who died overseas is a work which will go on indefinitely as America bends every effort to pay fitting tribute to those who gave their last full measure of devotion.* http://www.qmfound.com/graves_registration.htm

The American Graves Registration Service, directly under the quartermaster General, was charged with this massive effort for the identification and burial of "all army, navy, marine, and coast guard personnel who lost their lives as the result of service outside the continental limits of the United States." Other countries such as the UK has also been long involved in locating their unknowns.[52]

While every MIA unknown is tragic, the number from World War II is just overwhelming. But what is hopeful is that there have been many identified in the ensuing years. Records indicate that there were 78,750 missing in action at the end of the war in 1945, which represents about 19 percent of the total killed (405,399). This means that for every five killed in World War II, there was one MIA. One in five families had no closure for their loved son or daughter. A shocking statistic! However, it is very encouraging to learn that there have been 5,073 MIAs identified since 1945 or about eighty-five per year on average. There were ninety-eight MIAs recovered, identified, and returned home in 2011. Amazing to me was the fact that the Joint POW/MIA Accounting Command (JPAC) deploys many teams a year to search for, recover, and identify these heroes. JPAC has a state-of-the-art forensic lab in Hawaii, where discovered American unknown military remains are analyzed and identified.

Another government agency that communicates with families of still missing MIAs is the Defense POW/Missing Personnel Office (DPMO), whose motto is "Keeping the Promise." I have been in contact with DPMO, and they have been very helpful in my search. They recently conducted a thorough search and investigation into all of the currently available records that included the following:

- Individual deceased personnel file for Eugene F. Darter, S/Sgt, 39541802, Record Group 92: Records of the Office of the Quartermaster General, Washington National Records Center, Suitland, MD
- Missing aircrew report (MACR) 1558
- The missing aircrew reports of the US Army Air Forces, 1942-1947, National Archives Microfilm Publication M13380, Record Group 92
- Records of the Office of the Quartermaster General, National Archives, College Park, MD
- World War II Honor Roll listing for Eugene F. Darter, S/Sgt, 39541802, American Battle Monuments Commission (ABMC). http://www.abmc.gov/home.php
- Enlistment record for Eugene F. Darter, S/Sgt, 39541802, Electronic Army Serial Number Merged File, ca. 1938-1946, World War II Army Enlistment Records, Record Group 64: Records of the National Archives and Records Administration, National Archives, College Park, MD. Searchable database accessible from this Web address: http://aad.archives.gov.aad

DPMO sent me a detailed case summary report documenting everything they found related to my brother from these many documents from which I found new information. Had I just begun my search, obtaining all of these records would have taken me years and considerable travel expense to locate. So anyone beginning a search for their MIA has a valuable resource in DPMO. They can be contacted at

Department of the Army
US Army Human Resources Command
Past Conflict Repatriations Branch
1600 Spearhead Division Avenue
Fort Knox, KY 40122
Visit DPMO Web site at http://www.dtic.mil/dpmo
or call 800-892-2490

There are also privately funded, nonprofit organizations that conduct intensive searches for MIAs such as MIA Hunters and Moore's Marauders, who can be located on the Internet.

Given the difficult economic times we live in, the JPAC and DPMO, as well as the private agencies, represent an invaluable resource to families searching for their MIAs. The families that are so blessed with the identification of their loved one are incredibly thankful for this because no one can imagine the satisfaction of knowing finally where and how your loved one gave their life for their country. There are no words that could express how much this would mean to our family if Eugene's remains were to be discovered and brought home. Although the loss itself is tragic, the uncertainty involved in having a loved one remain MIA is agonizing over time. Being able to bring your loved one back home to be given their due honor helps enormously in the healing process.

Wil S. Hylton who spent five years documenting the mission and loss of the entire crew of a B-24 in the Pacific in a book called *Vanished*[51] wrote the following on July 11, 2013, in the *New York Times* magazine about MIA families like mine:

> *Families that experience a Missing In Action loss know how precious this work is. With no clear explanation for what has happened to their sons, fathers, husbands and brothers, they experience a distinct form of grief known as "ambiguous loss." Only a few experts have looked closely at the special trauma of M.I.A. families, and the way their suffering passes from generation to generation. In many cases, these families nurture hope that the man has somehow survived—that he's lost or captive or suffering from amnesia, even though these fates might be worse than death. I have met young men and women who are consumed by the loss of a grandparent they never knew, because his disappearance has loomed over their families for decades. For these M.I.A. families, there can be no real closure without a credible search for answers.*

Every week now, two or three notices are announced by DPMO and JPAC regarding the return of the remains of a US serviceman that have been identified to his family for burial with full military honors. Army Sgt. Charles L. Scott, twenty, of Lynchburg, Virginia, is a recent recovery. He became MIA in the Korean War in 1950, and in 1954, the United Nations and Communist forces exchanged the remains of the war dead in what came to be known as Operation Glory. Remains that were unidentifiable were interred at the National Memorial Cemetery of the Pacific, known as the Punchbowl in Hawaii. In 2012, scientists from the Joint POW/MIA Accounting Command (JPAC) reassessed the possibility of identifying the remains using modern technology, and the decision was made to exhume the remains for identification. In the identification of Scott, scientists from JPAC and the Armed Forces DNA Identification Laboratory (AFDIL) used circumstantial evidence and forensic identification tools such as dental comparisons, radiography comparisons, and mitochondrial DNA, which matched Scott's mother and sister. Amazing! National POW/MIA Recognition Day is held each year on the third Friday of September to commemorate the sacrifices of the missing and their families.

Grave marker for unknown US military personnel
(Photo credit M. I. Darter)

Identification of the Vietnam Unknown

I read a number of remarkable stories about the identification and recovery of MIAs over the past six decades. One of them shows that anything is possible regarding unknowns. An unknown from Vietnam was randomly selected from among many unknown remains, and an army caisson carried the Vietnam unknown from the Capitol to the Memorial Amphitheater at Arlington National Cemetery on Memorial Day, May 28, 1984, where the unknown was awarded the Medal of Honor by President Regan.

Ten years later, in 1994, Ted Sampley, a POW/MIA activist, determined through research that the remains of the Vietnam unknown were likely those of Air Force First Lt. Michael Joseph Blassie, who was shot down near An Loc, Vietnam, in 1972. Sampley published an article in his newsletter and contacted Blassie's family, who attempted to pursue the case with the Air Force's casualty office but with no action. In January 1998, CBS News broadcast a report based on Sampley's investigation, which brought political pressure to support the identification of the remains. The body was exhumed on May 14, 1998. Based on DNA testing, Department of Defense scientists confirmed the remains were those of Lt. Blassie. The identification was announced on June 30, 1998, and on July 10, Blassie's remains arrived home to his family in St. Louis, Missouri and reinterred nearby.[40] This is astonishing indeed and gave me, and I'm sure many others, some renewed hope.

Could My MIA Brother Be Found? A Very Cold Case!

Over the years, I wondered again and again what if anything could be discovered after so many years? I had zero hope that he could be found and brought home. His Purple Heart was in my possession, and I often held it in my hand and thought about him, but it always gave me a great feeling of sadness that we knew almost nothing about what had happened. My parents had given me their only photo of his crew (with no names) standing in front of their Flying Fortress, which I often looked at wondering what happened to him and all of his crewmates. We did not even know his bomb group unit. Could any of them still be alive after all these years? Is that possible? This was indeed a very cold case. The only face we recognized below was my brother's. Such good-looking young men, I wondered and wondered over the years if any of them survived the war and was alive today. Of course it would be foolish to even think that I could find out what happened to my brother and his crew members after more than fifty years.

Photo of my brother's B-17 crew in possession of our father. I looked at this photo many times and wondered if any had survived the war. While I did not know then, they were later identified as follows: Standing (L to R): Robert T. McKeegan, Doral A. Hupp, Loren E. Dodson, Charles J. Schreiner, Eugene F. Darter, and Frank V. Lee; Kneeling (L to R): Don P. Neff, Junius (Ed) Woollen, Royal L. Jackson, and Fred A. Delbern. (Photo credit United States Army Air Corps)

I had an extremely demanding career as a professor of civil and environmental engineering at the University of Illinois and a large family of five children, which left very little time to pursue what had become a continuing growing passion in my heart and mind about my brother that I had only met once on a pillow. But he was constantly in my mind whenever the topic of war came up or someone asked me if I had any siblings or whenever I watched a movie on World War II. During an engineering evaluation on a US Air Force base in the early 1980s, I came upon an old B-17 sitting on a hard stand. I walked around and around it, trying to see the inside and imagining by brother inside performing his duties as radio operator and gunner. Was he one of the three who bailed out? Or did he go down with the plane? I thought to myself that someday I will try to find out his fate. When the Berlin Wall came down and later some news reports of American soldiers found in graves in Eastern Germany circulated, it sent shivers down my spine, recalling my parents' insistence of him surviving the war and probably dying in a Soviet prison somewhere.

Miracles Still Happen, At Least on the Internet!

Then late one winter night at the office, on his January 3, 2000, birthday, my fingers, out of the blue, typed B-17 into Yahoo! Search, and what popped up on my screen filled me with an intense emotion that has only grown in intensity ever since to find out what happened to my brother. There appeared Web sites of several American units that flew B-17s from England to bomb Nazi targets all over Europe. In these Web sites were e-mails from loved ones searching for their fathers, uncles, grandfathers, brothers, and more, and there were answers from credible people. I went home very late that night and found that old yellow letter dated December 17, 1943, from the War Department, the Adjutant General's Office, Washington DC, that contained the B-17 serial number, my brother's serial number; the target, Bremen; and a brief message about the plane being hit.

> *The record concerning your son shows that he was a crew member of a Flying Fortress on a mission to Bremen, Germany, on 16 December 1943. His plane was attacked by enemy aircraft upon completion of the bomb run and was last seen losing altitude approximately twenty-nine miles west of Bremen.*[25]

I also found another old yellow letter dated May 14, 1946, Headquarters, American Graves Registration Command, European Theater Area, APO 887, US Army.

> *Aircraft B-17F, #42-30255 departed on a mission to Bremen, Germany, 16 December 1943. The aircraft is thought to have been hit by anti-aircraft fire just before reaching the target. The #3 engine was lost causing the plane to drop back out of formation. It continued over the target, dropped its bombs, losing altitude and dropping further behind the formation.*[23]

The next morning, I sent this information to a dozen random e-mail addresses that were on these Web sites. The first return e-mail the next day was from a daughter of an American airman whom she had never met because he was shot down and never found. Adrian Caldwell responded that if my brother was either buried overseas or MIA, he should be honored on a Wall of the Missing at an American cemetery in Europe. She gave me the Web site for the American Battle Monument Commission (http://www.abmc.gov/home.php) and said to enter by brother's name to see if they had a record.

I did this immediately, and to my utter amazement, up popped a Web page with his name and his unit (the 95th Bomb Group and the 412th Squadron). It also stated that he was honored on the Tablets of the Missing at Cambridge American Cemetery, England. I was absolutely stunned and amazed to see this information. Wow! I finally knew his bomb group and that he was honored on the Tablets of the Missing. I immediately arranged for a friend of a friend who was stationed at RAF Lakenheath nearby to visit the cemetery and take an etching and a photo of my brother's name on the wall.

THE WORLD WAR II HONOR ROLL

Eugene F. Darter

STAFF SERGEANT, U.S. Army Air Forces

Service # 39541802
412nd Bomber Squadron,
95th Bomber Group Heavy

Entered the Service from: California
Died: December 16, 1943
Missing in Action or Buried at Sea
Tablets of the Missing at
Cambridge American Cemetery
Cambridge, England

Awards: Air Medal, Purple Heart

My first discovery from the American Battle Monument Commission
(ABMC Web site, www.abmc.gov)

A few months later, I traveled to the UK and was standing in the beautiful cemetery in total awe. For me, that first visit to Cambridge American Cemetery was extraordinary. I walked along the long, high wall, searching the engravings for his name. There are over five thousand names, and when I found it, I walked up and ran my fingers through the letters over and over. It was surreal for me after so many years to be at the spot where my brother Eugene Darter was truly honored. Tears streamed down my face. The cemetery superintendent was incredibly kind and packed some brown sand from Normandy beach into the engraved letters. The photo below was taken of this very special moment.

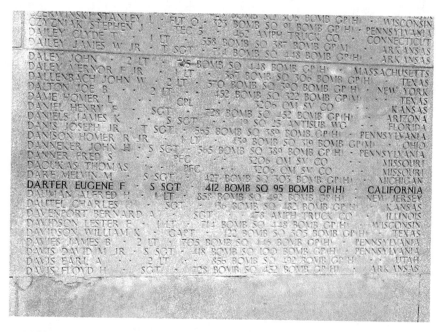

Tablets of the Missing, over five thousand names, Cambridge American Cemetery, England (managed by the American Battle Monuments Commission) (Photo credit M. I. Darter)

Along the long, high wall of the missing, there were several larger-than-life statues of a soldier, a sailor, an airman, and a coastguardsman. The Army Air Corps statue was not far from my brother's name on the wall. The larger-than-life statue became kind of a stand-in for Eugene, and every time when I visit Cambridge Cemetery, I stand alongside the airman statue, my "big brother," and give honor to him and thank him for what he did so that our family and countless other families could enjoy freedom in our lives.

Over many visits since, I noticed that many people come to Cambridge American Cemetery to pay homage to their family members who are honored here, especially on the US Memorial Day when there is a big ceremony honoring those buried there and those honored on the Wall of the Missing. It appeared that most of the MIAs on this wall were lost during the strategic bombing of Nazi Europe. This first visit, walking through the burial sites and along the wall and the beautiful chapel, increased my respect for these Americans who made the ultimate sacrifice. So many graves . . . So many names on the Wall of the Missing . . . Wow, there was Capt. Glenn Miller's name, who gave up the highest-paying musician salary in the world at that time in New York City to join up and organize an Air Force Band and play at American and British bases around England during the war to help boost morale. He was lost on his flight from England to Paris in December 1944, just two months after he played one of his last concerts at my brother's base. I also noticed Joseph Kennedy's name, older brother to President John F. Kennedy, who, after flying his twenty-five combat missions, volunteered for an extremely dangerous mission and was killed when his Liberator bomber blew up shortly after takeoff near the village of Blythburgh in Suffolk, England. The highly explosive load on the bomber was intended for Nazi war facilities at a French port.

Meeting my "big brother" Eugene Darter at Cambridge American Cemetery, UK
(Photo credit M. I. Darter)

I left Cambridge American Cemetery that day thinking, "What greater gift can a person give than to lay down their life for their country?" There is none. I also thought, "Now let's go find my brother and bring him home!"

CHAPTER 2

MEETING THE AIRMEN

The next e-mail response from my first B-17 search arrived the next day. This e-mail was from a World War II researcher whose name has been lost, but to whom I will be forever grateful because it provided an attachment that showed the record of a B-17F named the *Lonesome Polecat II* over twenty-one missions. The last mission of this Flying Fortress was to Bremen, Germany, on December 16, 1943. And most importantly, for the last mission, the names and hometowns of all ten crew members were given, and my brother was one of them.

230255 412 V Lonesome Polecat II			
1 May 43 Accepted into USAAF Inventory			
1 Jun 43 Assigned to UK			
10 Jun 43 Gained by 351BG			
16 Jun 43 Gained by 95BG			
28 Jun 43 First Operational Sortie			
28 Jun 43	A ex	RES	
4 Jul 43 D. M. Eastling	A 4	P	
10 Jul 43 J. A. Storie	A 10	P	
14 Jul 43 J. A. Storie	A 16	P	
17 Jul 43 D. M. Eastling	A 10	P	
26 Jul 43 D. M. Eastling	A 16	REM	
No Record			
28 Jul 43 J. A. Storie	A 7	P	
29 Jul 43 W. A. Baker	B 15	REM	
#1 oil tank leaking			
30 Jul 43 J. A. Storie	B 16	A	
12 Aug 43 J. A. Storie	A 16	P	
9 Sep 43 C. R. Stotesbury	A 1	P	
23 Sep 43 R. F. Fischer	A 14	P	
4 Oct 43 D. H. Merten		RFO	
Forced landing RAF Westcott			
14 Oct 43 W. V. Owen	A 3	P	
20 Oct 43 J. P. Casper	A 18	P	
3 Nov 43 J. R. Miller	A 10	A	
5 Nov 43 L. A. Wehrman	B 7	P	
13 Nov 43 J. R. Miller		RFO – B (to Bremen)	

BT	E. J. Castona	KIA	
LW	Charles O. Witbeck	KIA	?, Ohio
TG	James J. Cook	KIA	

30 Nov 43	T. R. Batcha	A 8	P
5 Dec 43	R. A. Woodcock	A 20	P
13 Dec 43	R. W. Holcombe	B 11	P

16 Dec 43	F. A. Delbern Jr		FTR

West of the target and with #3 feathered, this B-17F left the formation under control; crashed Texel, Holland - 4 KIA - 6 POW - MACR 1558.

P	2Lt Frederick A. Delbern Jr	KIA	Duluth, Minnesota
CP	2Lt Don P. Neff	KIA	Spokane, Washington (originally Dayton, Ohio)
N	2Lt Royal L. Jackson	POW	Hartland, Vermont
B	2Lt Junius E. Woollen	POW	High Point, North Carolina
TT	S/Sgt Loren E. Dodson	KIA	Greenfield, Illinois
RO	S/Sgt Eugene F. Darter	KIA	Long Beach, California
BT	S/Sgt Charles J. Schreiner	POW	Fargo, North Dakota
LW	S/Sgt Frank V. Lee	POW	Bulls Gap, Tennessee
RW	Sgt Doral A. Hupp	POW	Brookville, Ohio
TG	S/Sgt Robert T. McKeegan	POW	Philadelphia, Pennsylvania

Note: S/Sgt Loren E. Dodson was not KIA, but was POW. He lived in Carrolton, Illinois until his death in 2007.

Information from "Operational Record of the 95th Bomb Group (H),"
by Paul M. Andrews[14] about a B-17F #42-30255 named *Lonesome Polecat II*

I almost fell off my chair when I saw my brother's name, S/Sgt. Eugene F. Darter, KIA, and his nine crewmates hailing from all over the country. For a moment, time stood still as I began to realize what this meant. I was shocked, and I remember speaking aloud, "My god, are any of these men still alive?" They would all be in their eighties by now, so it is possible. My children thought they may be, and we jumped into www.whitepages.com and quickly located phone numbers for a couple of the names.

Seek and Ye Shall Find!

My first call went unanswered, but my second call was answered by a lady with a great Southern accent, and after I told her my name and that I was looking for a man named Doral Hupp who flew in World War II, she said, "Well, you're in luck. He's sitting right here on the sofa." Doral took the phone, and I asked him if he knew my brother Eugene Darter. I was stunned when he answered, "Yes, he was my crewmate, and I found him on the floor of the B-17 radio room bleeding profusely from his right arm and leg after being hit by an attacking Nazi fighter. I stopped his bleeding, gave him a painkiller, and got him up on his feet. He was weak from much loss of blood, but I attached his parachute on his chest."

Doral said they were all getting ready to bail out and that the plane was hit badly and one was engine on fire. Doral said that Eugene appeared white and weak but was able to walk once up on his feet. He then somehow squeezed by the ball turret and the crew who were frantically getting their parachutes and gear on. Eugene looked at Doral and somehow managed a partial smile and told them he would be all right. He immediately turned around and jumped through the rear side door that had been kicked open. Surprised, Doral and the other crew immediately looked out the side windows to see if his chute opened, which it did, but he quickly entered the thick undercast below the aircraft and vanished. Very shortly thereafter, Doral said that he and the remaining crew bailed out soon thereafter and also disappeared into the dense clouds below, expecting a freezing North Sea splash down and certain death.

Well, again tears streamed down my face, and I became very emotional as I had just found out what happened to my brother, or at least part of the story. Doral told me about two other crewmates, Loren Dodson from Carrolton, Illinois (who amazingly lived just two hours from where I lived and Charlie Schreiner who lived in Burbank, California.

After a long talk with Doral, I immediately called Loren and Charlie and had equally long emotional conversations with them. I was stunned at what I had discovered so quickly, but my desire for more knowledge of what happened to Eugene only increased. And I later found out that Doral, Loren, and Charlie were also stunned but very happy that someone was interested in finding out what happened to three of their crewmates whom they had prayed for every day in the prisoner-of-war (POW) camp and were greatly sorrowed when they never showed up after the war ended and all prisoners returned home.

I soon traveled to meet each of these three men and their wives and was just so impressed by all of them. They were such fine examples of the Greatest Generation. I became very close to each of these men and their lovely wives (all in their eighties) over the next five years. I of course took detailed notes at these interviews. The story they told me about the combat between their B-17 and the anti-aircraft guns on the ground and the German fighters in the air was shocking. Nearly all of the crew was wounded and the plane severely damaged and two engines shot out, with one on fire and lots of smoke.

2000

S/Sgt. Doral Hupp in 1943 (looking quite stressed) and in 2000 (looking much happier) when we first met. Doral initially saved my brother's life when he stopped his bleeding, got him up on his feet, and clipped his parachute on upside down so he could pull it with his left hand since his right arm was badly shot and unusable. (Photo credit M. I. Darter)

None of the crew knew what happened to Eugene after he bailed out and entered the clouds. In fact, they also did not know what happened to the two pilots, Fred Delbern and Don Neff, who were alone on the B-17 *Polecat* after they bailed out. They suspected that it soon exploded and crashed into the North Sea. Doral and Charlie told me that when they came through the thick fog below, they expected to splash down and quickly die in the North Sea. But when they broke through the undercast, there was land! A Dutch island named Texel out in the freezing North Sea and they had amazingly avoided certain death.

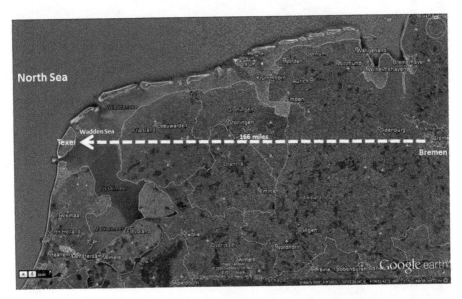

The western route taken by the 95th BG and far below the formation the struggling *Lonesome Polecat II* from Bremen, Germany, as it crosses the Wadden Sea and approaches one of the Frisian Islands, called Texel Island, the Netherlands (Image credit Google Earth)

I then began more detailed investigations to locate any other surviving crew members. I soon located Royal (Pete) Jackson in Tucson, Arizona, after the city hall in his hometown in Vermont put me in touch with his sister. Pete told me that he was blinded in one eye by a piece of flak just as he bailed out over Germany but was well treated in a German hospital and then imprisoned.

Later, I located the son and daughter of another crewmate, Ed Woollen, through Ed's brother James in North Carolina. Ed's son, John Woollen, and I talked by phone, and he told me his father had passed in 1986, but he had written a beautiful memorial to his three lost crewmates just after he was imprisoned by the Nazis, which he sent to me and is provided at the end of this story. John and I then discovered to our utter amazement that he and I were classmates in civil engineering graduate school at the University of Texas at Austin during the same years and we both had the same supervising professor, Ronald Hudson. Can you imagine that? We remember each other, but if we only knew then in the early 1970s what we know now . . . oh god, the wealth of information that I could have obtained from Ed would have been so valuable in the investigation of what happened to my brother and the pilots Delbern and Neff.

Finally, with Doral's help, we located Rosemary McKeegan, the wife of another crewmate Bob McKeegan, in Philadelphia; and she was able to tell me about his life and death in 1996. Doral told me how he worked with Frank Lee in Dayton, Ohio, at Wright Patterson AFB and of his death in 1984.

Crew of the *Lonesome Polecat II*, B17F

The crew of the *Lonesome Polecat II*, or just *Polecat* for short, included a mix of the vast melting pot of young men across the United States in 1943. A photo of the crew in their new leather jackets was shown in chapter 1, taken on their way to England in October 1943. The ten-man crew consisted of four officers and six enlisted men.

Lt. Fred A. Delbern (pilot) and Lt. Don P. Neff (copilot)
(Photos credit United States Army Air Corps)

The pilot, Lt. Fred A. Delbern, twenty-four years old, was from Duluth, Minnesota. Fred was an outgoing and happy student in high school and was an outstanding athlete excelling in football. He obtained a football scholarship to the University of Minnesota, where he played until the war broke out and he enlisted in the Army Air Corps. Fred was crazy about flying and had previously learned to fly a small single-seat aircraft. Ironically, I found Fred's name on the Cambridge American Cemetery just a few feet from my brother's name on the Wall of the Missing. Fred fell in love with Geraldine, and they married only a year before she kissed him good-bye in Spokane in November 1943, never to see him again.

Lt. Fred Delbern, Wall of the Missing, Cambridge American Cemetery, UK
(Photo credit M. I. Darter)

The copilot was Lt. Don P. Neff who was born in Bryan, Ohio, in 1917. Don loved flying, just like Fred, and fell in love with Marjorie Staley during his final training near Spokane and married her on October 7, just a few days before the crew departed for England. He became MIA two months later on December 16, 1943, at twenty-six years of age. Don and navigator Pete Jackson became best of friends during training. Pete told me that just before he bailed out, he climbed up to the cockpit and saw Don in the copilot's seat flying the stricken aircraft. They waved and smiled and said good-bye to each other. A memorial service was held for Don one year after he became missing in Montpelier. I found Don's name on the impressive large Wall of the Missing at Margraten American Cemetery in the Netherlands, and we have just recently found relatives of the Neff family in Ohio.

NEFF DON P
2 LT 412 BOMB SQ 95 BOMB GP (H)   OHIO

Lt. Don P. Neff, Wall of the Missing, Margraten American Cemetery, NL
(Photo credit M. I. Darter)

Lt. Royal (Pete) L. Jackson and Lt. Junius (Ed) Woollen
(Photo credit United States Army Air Corps)

Another officer in the crew included the navigator, Lt. Royal (Pete) L. Jackson, twenty-six, from Hartland, Vermont. Jackson and Neff became good friends and palled around together. I discovered Pete Jackson through his sister located in his hometown in Vermont. He was in a nursing home in Tucson, Arizona, in 2002, where he was suffering from Alzheimer's. Pete lived an adventurous life of traveling and exploring and had never married, but he whispered to me that he "came very close once." But Pete seemed to remember everything from his training and mission to Bremen.

As he bailed out, he was hit in the eye with a small piece of flak which blinded his eye, and he did not recall pulling his chute chord or landing. He woke up in a German hospital where they took good care of him until he was transferred to the Barth POW camp for officers. Pete said that he felt the German Luftwaffe (Air Force) had considerable respect for the American airmen (this respect was shown by both sides during the war but was not shown by the SS or Gestapo).

Photo of Royal (Pete) Jackson (left) from Vermont and Michael Darter when they met in 2003. Pete was the navigator on the *Polecat* and was hit in the eye just as he bailed out by flak. (Photo credit M. I. Darter)

The bombardier, Lt. Junius (Ed) Woollen, twenty-seven, was from Highpoint, North Carolina, and was born in 1916. Ed attended High Point College for two years and then received an appointment to the US Military Academy at West Point in 1937, which he attended for one year. Ed was hit on board and bailed out and became a POW for eighteen months. He stayed in the Air Force, serving his country for many more years. He died in 1986 in San Antonio, Texas.

S/Sgt. Charles J. Schreiner and S/Sgt. Frank V. Lee
(Photo credit United States Army Air Corps)

The left waist gunner, S/Sgt. Charles J. Schreiner, 29, was born in Fargo, North Dakota. He had previously escaped the harsh winters of North Dakota and moved to California and was working for Lockheed when he was drafted. He had a long career for Lockheed aircraft living in Burbank and visited and comforted Eugene's mother in Long Beach on several occasions. Charlie's injuries on the mission stayed with him throughout his life, and he was a POW for over eighteen months. He was very fortunate to have fallen in love with a wonderful woman named Vickii, who became his wife for over fifty years when he died in 2003. His detailed letter to Ms. Geri Delbern in 1945 was incredibly helpful in understanding what happened on their mission to Bremen.[36]

The right waist gunner was S/Sgt. Frank V. Lee from Bulls Gap, Tennessee. Frank was born in 1921 and was twenty-two at this time. After the war, he worked at Wright-Patterson AFB with Doral Hupp. Both Frank and Doral bailed out and landed near each other and were captured and became POWs for eighteen months. Frank was married and died in 1984 in Dayton, Ohio.

S/Sgt. Robert J. McKeegan (left) and S/Sgt. Doral A. Hupp
(Photo credit United States Army Air Corps)

From Philadelphia, Pennsylvania, came the skinny tail gunner, S/Sgt. Robert J. McKeegan, twenty-three. Bob was a most caring and loving man who never complained in his life according to his lovely wife Rosemarie, who said that they had a wonderful fifty-year marriage. She was his princess and he her prince. However, Bob's combat and eighteen-month POW experience did have a very stressful effect on him and caused him considerable anxiety in the later years.

The ball turret gunner was S/Sgt. Doral A. Hupp, twenty-three, born in Wirt County, West Virginia, but living in Brookfield, Ohio, when he joined the Army Air Corps. Hupp was just short enough to fit into the very tight ball turret, a position that one rarely survived in an emergency. Doral saved my brother's life temporarily on the aircraft and became a POW for eighteen months. He survived the war and married and had four children and a great career as a civilian auditor working for the US Marine Corps. He and his wife Winnie Hupp were married more than fifty years prior to his death in 2007. Doral is buried in Arlington National Cemetery.

S/Sgt. Loren E. Dodson (Left) and S/Sgt. Eugene F. Darter, best of friends.
(Photo credit United States Army Air Corps)

The flight engineer and top turret gunner was S/Sgt. Loren E. Dodson, 26, from Greenfield, Illinois. Loren grew up in an Illinois farming family and knew how to work hard. As the aircraft engineer, he spent many hours studying the mechanical operation of the B-17. Loren was hit on the top turret and became a POW and survived the war. He worked for McDonald-Douglas responsible for aircraft painting in St. Louis. He and his lovely wife Kathleen were married over 50 years when he died in 2007 within a week of his POW bunkmate Doral's death.

From sunny Long Beach, California, came the radio operator, S/Sgt. Eugene F. Darter, thirty. Eugene was a security business owner and also an undercover police officer for the government who investigated Communist activity in the LA area before the war. At thirty, Eugene was the "grandfather" of the crew, although Charlie at twenty-nine was "way up" there also. Loren and Eugene became the best of friends during training and spent many happy times together, with Eugene playing many jokes on Loren as well as other crewmembers.

For me, it was such an incredible privilege to meet and get to know well four of these men, their wives, and three other families of crew members who had passed on. There is no doubt that each of the crew members was changed forever from the events of their first and last combat mission in Germany, whether they were wounded, captured, and imprisoned for many months, or simply disappeared and never seen again. This book is dedicated to these ten brave men and the many other brave aircrews who sacrificed their lives to stop the murderous Nazi war machine.

Continuing the Very Cold Case Search

Meeting and interviewing the four surviving crew members and the family members of three others was fantastic, but their story was complicated and much more information was needed. Further research was conducted at the National Archives II in Silver Springs, Maryland, where I located the Missing Aircraft Crew Report[3] #1558 (which contained all information on their B-17 and what each surviving crew saw) and the Operations Report of the 95th Bomb Group for December 16, 1943[4], which provided a wealth of information on the mission in Bremen. From the US Total Army Personal Command, I obtained the Individual Deceased Personnel File[1] (IDPF) for Eugene, which included every sheet of paper related to my brother and his medical files. These provided a huge amount of information about what happened on that fateful mission to Bremen, Germany.

Then every year for a dozen years, I traveled (often accompanied by one of my children) to the UK to London, Duxford, Cambridge, and the tiny village of Horham where the 95th Bomb Group of the United States Army Air Corps was stationed. We also traveled to Texel Island, the Netherlands, many times to search for information, clues, eyewitnesses, stories, and historical documents and to knock on doors and more. We wrote newspaper articles and had TV North Holland do a special on my MIA brother, asking anyone who lived during the war and recalled hearing or seeing a bomber and crew member in December 1943 to please contact me.

Doral and I enlisted the able help of Johan Graas, President of the World War II Aircraft Recovery Association of the Netherlands. He was able to help us locate many valuable pieces of information, such as the biography of the German pilot who claimed the shoot down of my brother's B-17 that led closer and closer to discovering what happened to my brother and his two missing pilots. Bit by bit and piece by piece, we (my children, Johan, crew members, and many others) began to piece together what happened on the crew's first combat mission over Germany on December 16, 1943. I became much more hopeful over time with numerous discoveries occurring. But the story was very complex with differing stories about events. Onward!

Michael Darter and Johan Grass investigating the B-17 flight path
across Texel Island (Photo credit M. I. Darter)

CHAPTER 3

FORMING OF CREW, TRAINING, AND FLIGHT TO ENGLAND

The crew of the *Lonesome Polecat II* was first formed as part of the 95th Bomb Group at Ephrata, Washington, in August of 1943. Each of the crew members had either enlisted or was drafted and sent to basic training and then to special training schools specific to his specialty area (pilot, radio operator, airplane mechanics, gunner, navigator, bombardier).

S/Sgt Eugene F. Darter at radio school training in South Dakota winter 1942/43. Eugene had a photographic memory and could easily memorize codes and manuals said his crewmates (Photo credit M. I. Darter)

At Ephrata (also at Walla Walla) and then at Spokane, crew members underwent intensive training on the many aspects of flying their B-17. Flight engineer Loren Dodson said,

> *The Air Force was bringing in men from all over the country to fill the various positions on the plane (pilots, bombardiers, navigators, radio operators), and from these the members of a plane crew were chosen. Forming a crew was a slow process, trying to put together a team that was compatible. I really can't remember when our crew came together, but I do remember our train ride to Spokane, Washington, as a full crew. We arrived at Geiger Field in Spokane somewhere around the 15th or 20th of August, 1943. We were immediately given a 10-day furlough and had to be back about the 1st of September to really begin our combat training. This was really an enjoyable good time, the flying experience and getting to know each other and the friendships that we formed. I still look back to those days as one of the great parts of my life.[2]*

Crew camaraderie was strong, and they spent considerable time together in training, in the flight to England, and then several weeks at the base. All of the crew went home for a last visit with their families before their assignment overseas. This was the first and last time that I met my brother as he flew me around on a pillow. They then returned to their base for their combat training. In late October (28-31), the crew flew to Grand Island, Nebraska, where they were outfitted with new supplies, including clothing, parachutes, and life jackets. Eugene wrote his last letter to our parents during this time and mentioned that his photo in chapter 2 was taken "wearing the top part of my flying suit that I use going up there a lot closer to heaven than you have ever been!" Little did he know as to just how close to heaven they would all be in just a few weeks.

The crew was assigned to Europe and the Ferry Command who flew them to England. In early November, the crew was divided into two groups and climbed into two new B-17s and were among the first 95th crews taking the northern route to England. Prior to this, B-17s were flown a very long route south to Brazil and across to Africa and north to England. Eugene Darter, Fred Delbert, Don Neff, Pete Jackson, and Loren Dodson were on one plane; and Ed Woollen, Charlie Schreiner, Doral Hupp, Frank Lee, and Bob McKeegan were on the other.

Their long flight took them from Grand Island to Detroit (Michigan) to Bangor (Maine) to Gander Field, Newfoundland (crew member Doral Hupp says they were delayed a few days due to a three-foot snowstorm). As one of their B-17s was landing in Bangor, the pilot dragged the tail wheel through a fence at the end of the runway and scared them to death. This caused Fred Delbern so much concern that he kept on his parachute the entire flight to England. They left Gander Field at 9:00 p.m. and, after a long, cold, non-pressurized, and turbulent flight across the Atlantic Ocean, landed in Valley, Wales, the next morning very close to the Irish Sea. They felt fortunate as many stories exist of crews losing their way and crashing in Greenland or in the Atlantic Ocean.

Loren Dodson tells the story from there:

> *We took various trains headed for London. We arrived at the Liverpool train station in London, where we had to wait awhile for an English lorry to pick us up to take us to another station to catch a train to Horham. While we were waiting, Eugene Darter and I went outside to a small restaurant to get something to eat. We ordered the famous tea and crumpets. Not a real tasty choice. The tea was hot with milk in it, which I didn't care for, and the crumpets were hard and not much taste. We didn't have any English money so we gave the waitress some American money and she took what she wanted. The truck driver took us through the main part of the city—Trafalgar Square, past many of the famous London landmarks and of course through the bombing destruction. This would be our only time in London.*[2]

The sights and sounds of war-damaged London in November 1943 had a big impact on all of the crew as they saw for the first time the terrible reality of the war all around them. The crew finally boarded a train and headed, they thought, to their assigned base and the 95th Bombardment Group. However, they were in store for a little unpleasant surprise first. The crew was taken to the 100th Bombardment Group by mistake (the bloody One Hundredth). When they arrived, the guys in the 100th group told them they were very unlucky as the Germans focused on killing their B-17s due to a mistake that occurred. They told them that one of their damaged B-17s had lowered its wheels, which was an agreed sign of surrender; and when a German fighter flew up to it to take them to a landing strip to surrender, they shot it down. The B-17 had somehow lowered its wheels by mistake. The Germans then apparently signaled out the 100th Bomb Group when they could find them.[2]

Soon the crew discovered they were indeed assigned to the nearby 95th Bomb Group at Horham, England, and they felt very relieved after hearing this horror story. They then traveled the short distance to Horham through the beautiful English countryside and finally arrived at their 95th Bomb Group base from which they would fly their combat missions over Nazi Germany.

CHAPTER 4

95TH BOMBARDMENT GROUP, ARMY AIR FORCE BASE (#119), HORHAM, ENGLAND

T he total trip from Grand Island, Nebraska, USA, to their assigned UK base took ten days, arriving at Horham (Station 119) on November 10, 1943. Here they were assigned to the 412th Squadron in the 95th Bombardment Group. They immediately continued intensive training and preparation for their first combat mission.

Horham Army Air Force Base

Many airfields were built in East Anglia, England, in 1942-43 (nearly seventy in Norfolk and Suffolk) at distances of about five to twenty miles apart. Horham, Suffolk, was home to the 95th Bombardment Group (BG) of the US Eighth Air Force. The 95th BG consisted of about forty B-17s and many ground support units. Horham was a tiny ancient village of 150 people located eighty-two miles northeast of London and just twenty miles from the North Sea. A plaque at the old Horham 95th BG airbase reads,

> It started with maps at the Air Ministry. Areas of low level flat land with few obstructions were identified as suitable for airfields. The surveyors drove the stakes into the field. The bulldozers arrived. Hedgerows, trees and houses were removed. Trains and

trucks brought tons of rubble from the bomb damaged cities. The giant paving machines crawled across the landscape, laying the concrete runways. Within months, half a million cubic yards of concrete were laid. Miles of ditches were dug for electric cables, water pipes, drains and sewers. To get around an airfield site up to 10 miles of roads would be built. Living quarters were built in the surrounding countryside.[21]

Besides being the home of the distinguished 95th BG where over nine thousand servicemen and servicewomen served from 1943 to 1945, this village's claim to fame includes the visit of Capt. Glenn Miller and his famous Army Air Force Band that helped the 95th BG airmen and support crews celebrate their two-hundredth mission with an unforgettable concert and dance. This concert took place on September 10, 1944, in the T2 hangar (Col. Dave McKnight has a recording of this concert on CD) only three months before Glenn Miller also became MIA on a flight to Paris over the English Channel.[21] However, his remarkable music lives on today as the Glenn Miller orchestra continues to play many concerts around the world.[16]

95th Bomb Group (BG)

The 95th BG compiled an incredible record of strategic bombing missions of military and industrial targets, humanitarian food drops, ground support missions, D-Day invasion support missions, and POW retrievals after the war.

- The 95th BG was the only Eighth Air Force Bomb Group to receive an unprecedented three Presidential Unit Citation awards for extraordinary heroism in action against an armed enemy: August 17, 1943, (Regensburg mission); October 10, 1943, (Munster mission); and March 4, 1944, (Berlin first American daylight bombing mission). The 95th lost thirteen aircraft and 130 crew members on these three missions alone.
- The men of the 95th BG flew 321 combat missions from May 13, 1943, to April 20, 1945. They flew several repatriation missions to retrieve US POWs from their internment camps.[41] Finally, the 95th BG flew several missions to drop food to save

the starving people in the Netherlands.[41] On the last food-drop mission, one of the B-17s flew over a German flak battery which shot and hit an engine, and the aircraft went down just three miles from the English coast, killing most of the crew. This B-17 became the very last of thousands that were shot down over Europe in WWII.

- The 95th BG claimed 425 enemy aircraft destroyed which is the highest number by any Army Air Force Bomb Group in WWII.[17]
- The 95th BG was the first American Bomb Group to achieve a daylight bombing mission in Berlin on March 4, 1944. This historic mission resulted in not only their third Presidential Citation award but also an amazing centerfold photograph in *LIFE* magazine on March 10, 1944, of 95th BG crew members standing near and on their aircraft.
- The group lost 576 men killed in action/service (KIA), and of these, 176 are still missing in action (MIA) and presumed killed (imagine, one out of every three lost are still missing with still grieving families like mine).
- The group lost 805 men as POWs, sixty-four as internees (in neutral countries), sixty-one as evaders, and 171 wounded in action.
- Together with the 390th Bomb Group and the 100th Bomb Group, they formed the Thirteenth Combat Wing of the Eight Air Force.
- No mission was ever turned back by enemy resistance.[7, 8, 9]

On March 31, 1944, General Curtis E. Le May commended the 95th BG as follows:

It is my pleasure and privilege officially to commend the officers and men of the 95th Bombardment Group (H) for its outstanding achievement in successfully completing, from 13 May 1943 to 23 March 1944, 100 heavy bombardment missions against the enemy. Engaged in daylight aerial combat against a mighty foe armed with the world's most concentrated antiaircraft and fighter defenses, our bombers and crews each day are carrying the war home to Germany with increasing destruction to her war plants and installations. In this gigantic undertaking, no bombardment group has earned more enthusiastic praise than the 95th.[7]

The motto of the 95th BG was "Justice with Victory," as shown on the emblem painted on the old hospital building at Horham.[21]

"Justice with Victory" motto of the 95th Bomb Group
(Image credit 95th Bomb Group Heritage Association, UK)

The 95th BG consisted of many smaller subgroups as described in the 95th Web site (www.95thbg.org).[16] The 95th BG Memorials Foundation was formed several years ago in the US "to educate the public regarding the history of the 95th Bomb Group and its role in the air campaign over central Europe during World War II, to promote the study and recognition of the total involvement of the aircrews and their related support units, and to provide and maintain appropriate recognition of all members of the 95th Bomb Group who gave up their lives in the successful effort to preserve freedom as their legacy to future generations." The 95th BG Memorials Foundation is very active today, being led by the descendants and others of the original veterans in carrying out this mission.

The 95th BG Heritage Association in the UK[17] also has an excellent Web site (www.95thbg-horham.com) and promotes the memory of the men and women who served at Horham with the 95th BG. This association is also very active today as described in chapter 20. These two Web sites have a tremendous amount of valuable information and are highly recommended for anyone interested in more details about the

95th BG. Of course, a lot of credit of the success goes to the support groups at Horham, including those who worked day and night in all kinds of weather to keep the B-17s flying. By all accounts, they were incredibly dedicated people.

The most recent comprehensive and up-to-date book on the 95th BG is titled *The Wild Blue Yonder and Beyond* by Rob Morris with Ian Hawkins, Potomac Books, 2012.[41] The book contains many stories of the incredible bravery displayed by the men of the 95th BG despite very heavy losses during the war.

The crew was assigned to the 412th Squadron that consisted of about ten B-17s, which was one-quarter of all B-17s on the base at that time. The other three squadrons were the 334th, the 335th, and the 336th. An aerial photo of the Horham runways, taxiways, and hardstands is shown below. B-17s are lined up on the main runway 25/07 where they took off mission by mission to take the war to the enemy a year before Allied troops came ashore at D-Day.[21] Yes, the tiny peaceful ancient village of Horham was on the front lines of the air war over Nazi-controlled Europe from June 1943 until the end of the war two years later.

Intense Preparation for the First Mission and the Dangers Involved

The crew spent the next few weeks in intense preparation for their first combat mission, which was soon upon them. Then just nine days after their arrival, a tragic event occurred that shocked all of them. They were watching the mission takeoffs on the morning of November 19 when the last B-17 commanded by Lt. K. B. Rongstad's lifted off the main Horham runway, made too sharp of a turn before reaching sufficient altitude, and lost lift and suddenly fell as its left wing hit the ground and exploded in a ball of fire and black smoke near the village of Redlingfield, damaging a nearby home. Inside the home were Ruby Gooderham, who was within a few weeks of giving birth, and her two-year-old daughter Ann. Both mother and daughter were knocked down by the blast but survived, and the baby boy was born less than a month later in good condition. However, none of the ten unfortunate crewmen in the aircraft survived. This tragic event had a very chilling effect on the new Delbern crew. This was dangerous work indeed.[7,41]

During this time at Horham, Loren Dodson recalled an event that occurred.

> There is one thing that happened while there that stands out in my mind. Some of our crew was at headquarters building one day just looking around. I don't remember who all was in the group; I remember Eugene Darter, Eddie Woollen, and myself but I don't recall the others. We stopped at a desk that had 3 index cards files on it. These files were about 2 feet long; two of them were filled and the other one about half full with names of those who were lost in the past missions. Eddie thumbed through them and turning to us said, "This doesn't look a bit good." Was this an omen of what was soon to happen?[2]

Their fears were well founded. By the time the crew flew its first combat mission on December 16, 1943 (the 95th BG had been in operation for over six months), and had lost sixty-one B-17s in sixty-one missions or an average of one per mission. This was a 4 percent loss rate of the total number of B-17s that took off on these missions. Approximately 610 crew members were either killed or missing or became POWs listed on those index cards to date the crew saw in the 95th BG headquarters. One mission over Kiel, Germany, resulted in ten out of twenty-six B-17s lost containing one hundred crew members, all on one day of the war.

During the summer and fall of 1943, each crew member was required to fly twenty-five combat missions for his tour of duty. This meant that for every one hundred crewmen of the 95th BG, the first twenty-five missions flown beginning in May 1943, only sixty-five would have survived, and thirty-five would have been either killed or missing or became POWs, and a small few would escape capture.

Aerial view of Horham airfield

Horham airfield, UK, home of the 95th Bombardment Group, US Eight Air Force during World War II (note: B-17s lined up on main runway and adjourning taxiways) (Photo credit United States Army Air Corps)

Several authors including Jeffrey Ethel in his book *Bomber Command* stated that to be in a bomber over Germany (daylight missions) during the summer and fall of 1943 was the most dangerous spot in all of the US services whether marine, navy, or army.[5]

> *Nevertheless, in spite of severe testing of even the highest morale, particularly during the summer and fall of 1943, American bomber crews did their jobs day after day, going up against the roughest flak and fighter defenses ever conceived. Because prewar planners believed bombers could get through without fighter protection had a great deal to do with the number of American losses.*
>
> *American bomber losses dropped from 9.1 percent per mission in October 1943 to 3.5 percent in March 1944 as long-range fighters (P-51) engaged the Luftwaffe fighter's intent on getting to the bombers.*

In spite of prewar faith in the ability of bomber formations to protect them from fighter attack, the opposite proved to be the case. Statistically the most dangerous place to be in combat that year, whether on the ground or in the air, and regardless of theater, was inside a bomber over Germany, USAF.

Examining the actual numbers shows that over twenty-six thousand US airmen were killed in the daylight air war over Europe from the Eighth Air Force from 1942 through 1945. There were fifty-five thousand UK airmen killed but over a longer period of time (1939 to 1945). By contrast, there were 24,511 US Marines killed in World War II.

The Eighth Air Force fact sheet provides the following information[42]:

- *By mid-1944, Eighth Air Force had reached a total strength of more than two hundred thousand people (it is estimated that more than 350,000 Americans served in Eighth Air Force during the war in Europe.)*
- *At peak strength, Eighth Air Force could dispatch more than two thousand four-engine bombers and more than one thousand fighters on a single mission. For these reasons, Eighth Air Force became known as the Mighty Eighth.*
- *The Mighty Eighth compiled an impressive record in the war. This achievement, however, carried a high price. Half of the US Army Air Force's casualties in WW II were suffered by Eighth Air Force (more than forty-seven thousand casualties, with more than twenty-six thousand dead).*

Therefore, if approximately twenty-six thousand were killed out of 350,000 total servicemen in the Eighth Air Force, this is a percentage of 7.4. For the 95th BG, there were 576 killed out of approximately nine thousand total service people, which gives a percentage of 6.4 percent. How does this compare with other branches of the US military during the war?

- Worldwide Army Air Force was 2.5 percent (88,119 out of 3,400,000).
- Marine Corps was 3.7 percent (24,511 out of 669,100)

- Navy was 1.5 percent (62,614 out of 4,183,446).
- Army (including the Army Air Force) was 2.8 percent (318,247 out of 11,260,000).[43]

The overall average for all branches was 2.5 percent. Thus, the statements found in various publications that a US airman over Europe (7.4 percent) had a higher percentage of service persons killed than any other branch of the US military appears to be sadly correct. In fact, these numbers show the percentage was over twice as high as the marine corps, the navy, and the entire army. The Eighth Air Force 7.4 percent death rate puts the concern of the *Polecat* crew about the losses in their unit into perspective. However, realizing to some degree the large risks they were about to undertake, the crew to a man just focused on intensive training without complaint to be ready when called for their first mission.

The crew did have some moments of fun, however. Eugene's best friend, top turret gunner and engineer Loren Dodson, continues,

> *Thanksgiving we had a turkey dinner. When we were served, Eugene got the neck with a little of the breast on it. It was the longest turkey neck I've seen. It looked as if the neck was about all that turkey had. Eugene was very amused and the rest of us were beside ourselves and we let him know it.*[2]

Eugene was quite a tease for this rather serious crew. When Charlie was promoted to a staff sergeant in England, Eugene sowed his stripes on his underwear. Eugene would also short-sheet some of the guy's beds and played some other practical jokes on them to break the tension. Eugene sent his last letter home near this time, telling his father "Happy Birthday" and that he loved him dearly, from "Somewhere in England".

The base hospital and NCO Club have been restored today as quite amazing living museums.[21] The Horham base had nice mess halls, an officer's mess, and enlisted men's mess halls. The airmen had places where they could have drinks and relax after a mission. The Red Feather Club was for the enlisted men (NCO) to relax and have a drink. The officers had the officer's club. Some of the men also went to local bars when there was no mission the next day.

Horham was a great base to many of the men who survived the war. They had hot water and hot showers. Each squadron has its own area of Quonset huts, and officers had barracks, but it was late November, and the cold weather had set in. It is rumored that some of the crew members of the *Lonesome Polecat II* were not satisfied with the poor quality of coal provided for the stoves in their Quonset hut. They decided to procure better coal from an off-limits area on the base. To do this, they foolishly risked all by scaling a fence, filled a box with coal, and then scaled back over and made it to their quarters without getting caught and enjoyed a little more warmth as winter set in. Some of the crew visited the Red Feather Club and partook of the libations there. Photographs of some of the amazing murals in the club that still exist and are on display today are shown in chapter 20.

The crew continued to train and prepare for their first combat mission. Most importantly, they learned about formation flying, firing their 50-caliber machine guns in formation, and many other things. On December 11, 1943, Ed Woollen and Frank Lee went on a mission to Emden, Germany as fill-in crew and may have gone on an additional mission. On the Emden mission, their B-17 barely returned with two engines shot out. The other crew members' first mission was not until December 16, but that day for which they had endured many months of training was suddenly upon them.

My visits to the old base at Horham, England, were always quite emotional, trying to find out where Eugene was stationed, where he took his meals, and especially where his B-17 was stationed on the airfield. Below shows Art Watson, a 95th BG technical specialist veteran stationed at Horham who clearly remembered the *Lonesome Polecat II* due to its many hazardous missions when it was badly shot up. He took me to the airfield location (right next to the village of Horham) where the *Polecat* stood, and we walked down the still-existing taxiway it would have taken to reach the end of the main runway on its last mission. We could only imagine what the crew was thinking on that fateful morning.

Standing where the huge T2 Hanger once stood where Glenn Miller played
a big two-hundredth mission concert just before he became missing over
the English Channel are Michael Darter, 95th BG veteran Art Watson (who
attended the Miller concert and knew the *Lonesome Polecat II*), Frank Sherman
(local young resident during the war), and Cornelius Ellen
(from the Netherlands). (Photo credit M. I. Darter)

CHAPTER 5

MISSION TO BREMEN, GERMANY, DECEMBER 16, 1943

Twelve Combat Wings of the Eighth Air Force made a highly concentrated attack on the large North Sea port of Bremen. Bremen is in northwestern Germany and was a major shipbuilding and industrial city. There were submarine facilities (the largest producer of 750—and 1,200-ton Nazi submarines which had sunk many Allied ships) beside the River Weser, about thirty miles from the North Sea. This was Germany's second largest port, and the target was the heavily strengthened U-boat construction facilities. This mission was reported in newspaper accounts as the largest raid of the Eighth Air Force to date. Heavy cloud cover was reported over the target. The Bremen area had several important military targets because the 95th BG had been there on four previous missions.[9]

Because of its critical military value, Bremen was defended by hundreds of flak batteries as well as many fighter bases. Given such formidable defenses, why did the United States insist on daylight bombing of Germany? From the beginning, the British had argued against daytime bombing missions because they saw the German Luftwaffe suffer serious losses over Britain in 1940 during daylight attacks and they themselves had suffered very heavy losses during their daylight attacks over Germany, which they had stopped. But the American command was committed to the concept of "precision bombing" during the daylight hours. In addition, they argued that the B-17 was armed to the teeth with ten .50-caliber machine guns and the supposedly precise

Norden bombsight that made it possible to "drop a bomb in a pickle barrel," which in the stormy skies over Germany proved to be not so accurate. The issue was settled in September 1942 when the US and RAF commands agreed to go ahead with a program of around-the-clock bombing (RAF at night and US by day).

However, the German defenses had grown much stronger than the US command anticipated. It appeared that in the fall of 1943, Germany was making an all-out effort to stop the US daylight bombing offense that continued to grow in size. Thus, it must have been having an increasing impact on the ability to continue the war. Between very fast shooting and devastating 88-mm antiaircraft guns (3.5 inches in diameter that could destroy a B-17 with a direct hit) on the ground and thousands of capable German fighter aircraft with well-trained and dedicated pilots in the fall of 1943, the daylight missions took heavy casualties, in one case as high as ten of twenty-six B-17s lost (38 percent) over Kiel, Germany, on one day of the war. Making matters much worse, during this time in 1943, the US fighter escorts did not have the fuel range to fly the entire mission into Germany to protect the bombers, leaving them vulnerable to hundreds of German fighters the moment the US fighter escort had to turn back to their bases to fuel up.[10, 18]

On this day, four Combat Wings of the First Bombardment Division, three of the Second Division, and five of the Fifth Division (mission report of the 95th BG for December 16, 1943) took off from many bases in the UK headed out over the North Sea for Bremen, Germany. This included 631 aircraft, one of which was an old warrior named the *Lonesome Polecat II*, a B-17F model (#230255, note that the precise identification is #42-30255) on its twenty-second combat mission.[4]

Early Morning, December 16, 1943

On this cold and foggy Thursday morning, the crew was awakened before sunrise (0500 hours) for their first combat mission. Hupp got up extra early and went and had breakfast by himself. All of the crew members were anxious preparing for their first mission. A few days before, they had to go through the personal effects of another crew (to ship home) that did not return from their mission.

0730 Hours: Preparation for Mission

After breakfast, when they arrived at their separate briefing rooms (for officers and enlisted men) and the CO pulled back the cover, the target was announced as the "Bremen port area." A collective groan went up from the 95th BG crews. Bremen was well known by the veteran crews (Bremen became known as "little B" as compared to the big "B" Berlin). Bremen was known to have the most intense and accurate enemy flak and fighter defense of the Third Reich at the time. It was called flak city by these crews due to the hundreds and hundreds of 88-mm antiaircraft guns surrounding the city. There were also plenty of enemy fighter bases on the way in and out of the city. Berlin would be coming up for the 95th BG on March 3, 1944, when they would become the first American bombers to bomb Berlin by daylight, receiving a Presidential Citation for the achievement as well as a centerfold photo of the crews in *LIFE* magazine. But first, some critical targets around Bremen had to be taken out.

A description of the flak by the pilot of the *Memphis Belle* on a mission over Bremen several months before noted that "the sky below us and around us was a boiling black lagoon of exploding metal."[10] This was to be the sixty-first mission of the 95th BG, which would fly more than three hundred missions from May 1943 to May 1945.

After breakfast, the crew obtained all of their equipment and climbed on a truck that took them to an "old" warrior bomber named the *Lonesome Polecat II*. This aircraft was named by one of its first pilots John A. Storey after the *Lonesome Polecat I* (#42-29693) from the same 412th squadron to which Storey belonged.[20] The *Lonesome Polecat I* was piloted by Lt. M. B. MacKinnon and was hit after four passes of a German Messerschmitt Bf 109 aircraft piloted by German Ace Lt. Heinz Knoke as they were returning from a mission over the North Sea on June 11, 1943. Knoke was credited with shooting down thirty-three Allied aircraft (nineteen of which were heavy bombers). The B-17F fell out of formation and exploded, falling into the sea, sadly killing all crew.[15] John Storey recalled to me how depressing it was at the missing crew quarters that night. A new B-17F aircraft #42-30255 was received by the 95th BG at Horham five days later and was named the *Lonesome Polecat II* by Lt. Storey and began flying missions over enemy territory on June 28, 1943.[14]

Between this date and December 16, 1943, the *Polecat* went on twenty-one bombing missions over Europe, with a forced landing at RAF

Westcott. In fact, two airmen were killed in action on board the *Polecat* during a mission on November 13 to, ironically, Bremen.

What was to unfold for the *Polecat* and her young crew was somewhat similar to what happened to the *Memphis Belle* (one of the most famous B-17s) eight months prior over the same well-defended target of Bremen. The mission of the *Memphis Belle* and her crew over Bremen is described by her pilot Col. Robert Morgan[10] and portrayed in the 1990 Warner Bros. movie of the same name.[12] However, while the *Memphis Belle* was shot up badly, it made it back to England, but the *Polecat's* story ended differently.

No photo of the complete *Polecat* exists, but the photo below is of a B-17F from the 95th BG (note the block *B* on the tail) with a serial number that is very close to the *Lonesome Polecat II*. Note that this aircraft was returning from a mission on October 9, 1943, and over the North Sea, the #2 engine was hit (note fire at the back of the #2 feathered engine) with the loss of all crew members moments after this photo was taken.[34] A similar situation is about to unfold for the old warrior *Polecat* and her crew on their first mission.

Photo of "Roger the Lodger" B-17F from the 95th BG with a serial number close to the *Lonesome Polecat II*, would have looked almost identical (note the feathered engine #2 with gasoline fed fire bursting out behind it, this B-17F blew up just minutes after this photo was taken, killing all crew over the North Sea).[8,21] (Photo credit United States Army Air Corps)

Lt. John Miller was one of the early pilots of the 95th BG and the *Polecat* and had a very harrowing mission over Bremen, Germany, on November 13, 1943, just four weeks prior to the December 16, 1943, mission. Amazingly, I was able to locate and interview John Miller in Madison, Wisconsin, in 2006 just before he passed on. He well remembered the *Polecat* and this particular mission as it was extremely harrowing as described below from a newspaper article graciously provided by John (which he obviously had a hand in writing just after the event, somehow getting the story back to Madison).

Fortress "Lonesome Polecat II" Torn to Shreds, Two Members of Crew dead, Make it Home

The LP II floundered helplessly behind a formation of heavy bombers raiding Bremen Sunday, with one of her engines knocked out, her entire tail section in shreds, and bearing gaping holes from nose to stern. A flock of ME 109s dived in for the kill, pumping 20-mm shells into the stricken bomber like rain beating on a tin roof. Two crew members already were dead, and one wounded. It looked like curtains for "Lonesome" and her crew—but she got home by a ruse. In desperation, pilot Capt. John Miller, 23 of Madison, Wis., broke off violent evasive action and threw the Fortress into a long steep dive featured by deliberate, wobbly gliding turns to the right and left, simulating a bomber heading for a crash. For 15,000 ft. "Lonesome" fluttered down like a leaf from a tree. The Jerries, probably sobered by the loss of three fighters to "Lonesome's" gunners, apparently believed the Fortress was crashing, and abandoned the chase. But the ship floundered to the protection of low-handing clouds and then struggled home across the North Sea at 1,500 ft., bucking a headwind which at times reached 80 mph.

Tears welled in the eyes of some of the eight surviving members as they told how the little tail gunner whose identity was as well as that of the dead waist gunner must remain undisclosed until their families are notified, died with both hands still gripping his gun handles, his head slumped over the gunsight, and still kneeling on one knee in battle position. They told of the waist gunner also killed instantly when a cannon shell hit him in the abdomen as he was firing at an oncoming fighter. He scorned wearing a flak suit, protesting that the protective armor was too heavy. He'd be alive today if he had worn it, a buddy said. Flak knocked out the number three engine as "Lonesome" started her bomb run. Oil from it spurted back against the bomber freezing in the 50 below zero temperature. The Fortress was knocked out of formation and 15 to 20 enemy fighters swarmed in, attacking from all sides. Sgt Robert J. Cupp, 24, of Uniontown, PA acting bombardier, could not release the explosives because of battle damage, and after a hard struggle the pilot salvoed them with emergency mechanism as he tried desperately to retain his position in the formation. The gunners were pouring it on the fighters. The tail gunner bagged one which exploded 100 yards away. "I got him! I got him" he excitedly over the interphone. That was the last the crew heard from him. That German fighter was the kid's sixth. He had already won the distinguished flying cross for destroying five.

After the ship landed (at Horham, England), one engineering officer took one look at the battered "Lonesome," and said he had never seen a bomber shot up so badly. Some holes in it were two ft. in diameter. Miller has been recommended for silver star awards.[49]

Yes, the *Lonesome Polecat* was one tough old bird. And just four weeks later, here comes another mission over Bremen with so many antiaircraft batteries on the ground and surrounding German airfields with ace pilots in the air. Oh my god!

0810 Hours: Crew Meets the *Polecat*

The men checked out their equipment and then trucked out to their assigned plane. It was still dark, and it was a very cold and overcast day when the crew arrived at the parked B-17F. The *Polecat* was parked on its hardstand loaded with fuel, ammunition, and bombs by the grounds crew. The crew looked her over, noting the *Lonesome Polecat* nose art (a familiar cartoon of the day) along with hundreds of patched holes, and loaded their gear and guns on board, boarded the huge bomber, checked out their guns, radio, and all instruments and navigation equipment, and prepared for the dangerous mission ahead of them.

Records show that the *Polecat* was loaded with eight five-hundred-pound demolition bombs, twenty one-hundred-pound incendiary bombs, and seven thousand rounds of caliber 50 AP. They also had the following 50-caliber machine guns: lower turret, upper turret, left and right waist positions, radio room, left nose, right nose, and tail.[4]

This was the first mission in combat for the Delbern crew. Since they had arrived in England, they had not flown many practice missions in tight formation flying either. They had to face this extremely dangerous mission to Bremen alone with the flying and defensive skills learned to date, but as Doral, Loren, Charlie, and Pete told me, they were prepared to give it everything they had. And given the hundreds of antiaircraft guns and enemy fighters surrounding Bremen, there was no doubt it would require everything they had.

0837 Hours: Polecat and Crew Depart for War over Germany

One by one, the huge bombers started their engines, generating a tremendous noise as all four squadrons of the 95th BG prepared for takeoff. On signal, each bomber left its concrete hardstands, moved along the perimeter taxiways, and approached the takeoff end of the main runway 25/07 as shown below.[21] The Fortresses began their take-off roll at about thirty-second intervals. In turn, the *Polecat* piloted by Lt. Fred Delbern and Lt. Don Neff started its engines and moved down the perimeter taxiway and finally out to the main Horham runway, fully loaded with ten crew, guns and ammo, equipment, fuel, and bombs. At 0837 hours, the old *Polecat* began its takeoff roll into the wind toward its twenty-second combat mission. As the heavily loaded aircraft picked up speed down the concrete runway apprehension was high among the crew.

One by one, the huge bombers took off from their Horham, England, base,
on the front lines of the horrific air war over Europe.[8, 21]
(Photo credit United States Army Air Corps)

As the *Polecat* reached the proper speed and Lt. Delbern pulled back on his controls, the heavily loaded aircraft shuddered and lifted off the runway, and the crew was on their way. They were full of both excitement and anxiety over their first dangerous combat mission. For this moment, they had endured countless hours of training. They had also watched over the past four weeks at Horham as one B-17 crashed on takeoff, killing all crew, and also saw that several 95th crews failed to return from their combat missions over enemy territory. Doral, Charlie, and Loren told me that while the men realized they were in grave danger, they just got down and carried out their duties without question or complaint. The fully loaded B-17F (sixty-four thousand pounds) required most of the six-thousand-foot main Horham runway to get off the ground.

A B-17F takes off from the main runway at the Horham, England, base of the 95th Bombardment Group on a mission.[8, 21] (Photo credit United States Army Air Corps)

0837 to 1101 Hours: Assembly over UK and Delay

The 95th Bomb Group was divided for this mission into Group A and Group B of eighteen and twenty-two aircraft each. All B-17s took off as scheduled between 0825 and 0911, with a one-thousand-foot ceiling and two-mile visibility. They climbed through a thick overcast sky until they reached the rendezvous altitude. However, they were delayed a long time circling in the air, and it was not until 1101 when they finally left the English coast en route to the target.[4]

1101 Hours: Departure from English Coast

The flight plan shows the course taken by the 95th as they flew out over the North Sea to a turning point.[3] Loren Dodson recalls,

> *After take-off, we found our place in the formation and then began the spiral climb for altitude for the flight to the target. It was a beautiful sight when we broke through the clouds; the bright sunshine above and the silver clouds below and the sight of so many planes in the sky.*[2]

The general flight plan was to take off from Horham, assemble over England, travel northeast out over the North Sea, turn sharply, and then come south over the target at Bremen. The B-17 squadrons formed and then headed to the target as shown below. The return flight plan was directly west from Bremen over Texel Island, Netherlands, and then back across the North Sea to their Horham base.

95th Bombardment Group streaming out on a mission over the Third Reich (note the contrails, which are the condensation trail left behind when hot humid air from the engine exhaust mixes with the thin cold air, which is similar to the cloud you see when you exhale and "see your breath")[8,21]
(Photo credit United States Army Air Corps)

The bombers were supposed to be escorted over enemy territory by P-47s, P-38s, and P-51s (one of the first P-51 missions) of the Eighth Fighter Command (the 4th, 355th, and 356th fighter groups). However, none of the escort appeared either for the inbound flight or for the first fifteen terrifying minutes after the target was bombed when the 95th Bomb Group was hit hard by enemy aircraft. The 95th mission report states that adverse weather and delays again hindered the location of the bombers by the fighters.[4] The delays and missed rendezvous turned out to be fatal for the *Polecat* and her rookie crew. This was particularly unfortunate as it was one of the first missions that utilized the long-range P-51 that carried sufficient fuel to fly with the bombers throughout the mission to protect them from enemy aircraft attacks.

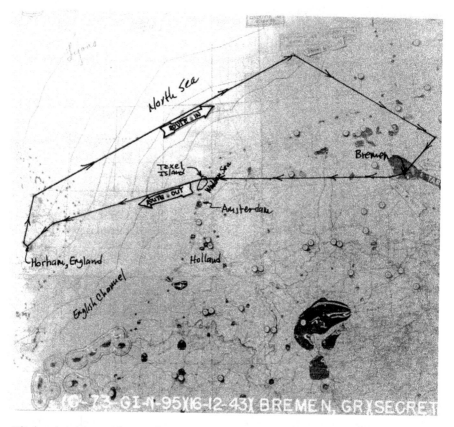

Flight plan into and out of Bremen, Germany, on December 16, 1943. Note that on the way out, the flight plan took the formation over a Dutch island named Texel. (Image credit United States Army Air Corps)

1110 Hours: Begin Climb to Bombing Altitude

The 95th began the climb to bombing altitude at 1110 (Group A) and 1125 (Group B). Approaching an altitude of ten thousand feet, pilot Delbern ordered the crew to go on oxygen. Without oxygen for even one minute, an airman can become unconscious. After twenty minutes, he'd be dead. And this unfortunately happened several times on missions. They reached the twenty-four-thousand-foot (A) and 23,600-foot (B) bomb altitude at 1232, which is nearly five miles straight up. The temperature at this altitude is very, very cold (e.g., -50 degrees F), and the crew began to feel its impact, especially the waist gunners Lee and Schreiner standing at open air side windows manning their guns and watching for enemy fighters to attack, Darter manning his 0.5-caliber gun out the open air top hatch of the radio room, Hupp in the ball turret, Dodson in the top turret, and McKeegan far back into the cold tail of the aircraft manning the twin tail guns. B-17s are neither heated nor pressurized. At this elevation, the extremely cold temperature can cause serious problems with the crew. Interestingly, none of the surviving crew recall being cold on this first mission. They were obviously focused on survival. From then on into the target, a close formation was maintained by all of the wings as they waited anxiously for the onslaught of flak and enemy fighters.

The position of the *Polecat* in Group B formation is shown below.[4] The formation is arranged so that the gunners can cover the sky in all directions. They were, however, in the low squadron at the end, which was the usual location assigned to a rookie crew (Loren Dodson called this the Purple Heart position). The enemy aircraft attacked this vulnerable position very often because it had the least coverage assistance available from other B-17 gunners. The enemy aircraft constantly to damage and then separate a bomber from the rest of the formation and finally destroy it. This was the plight of the *Polecat* on that day.

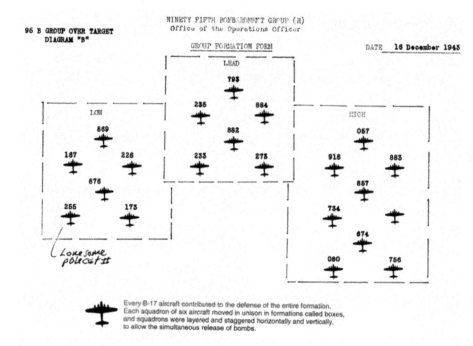

NINETY FIFTH BOMBARDMENT GROUP (H)
Office of the Operations Officer

GROUP FORMATION FORM   DATE   16 December 1943

95 B GROUP OVER TARGET DIAGRAM "B"

Every B-17 aircraft contributed to the defense of the entire formation. Each squadron of six aircraft moved in unison in formations called boxes, and squadrons were layered and staggered horizontally and vertically, to allow the simultaneous release of bombs.

Position of the *Lonesome Polecat II* B-17F (#42-30255) in the 95th B Group formation over Bremen, Germany.[4] Every B-17 aircraft contributed to the defense of the entire formation. Each squadron of six aircraft moved in unison in formations called boxes, and the squadrons were layered and staggered horizontally and vertically to allow the simultaneous release of bombs (lead group was at 23,000 feet, high group at 23,500 feet, low group at 22,500 feet). (Photo credit United States Army Air Corps)

1251 to 1302 Hours: German Coast to Initial Point

The enemy coast was crossed at 1251, and Group A reached the Initial Point (IP) of the bomb run at 1302, and Group B reached the IP just a minute later. The entire target area and the surrounding country were completely obscured by a heavy stratum of clouds, the top of which is estimated by the crews to be between four thousand and seven thousand feet.[4]

Photo of some B-17s of the 95th Bomb Group showing the target area black
smoke rising near Bremen on December 16, 1943 (this may be a photo
of the lower squadron where the *Polecat* was positioned).[4]
(Photo credit United States Army Air Corps)

The 95th Bombardment Group was the second bomber group over
the target, and there were many groups behind in the miles-long bomber
stream of over six hundred aircraft. Loren Dodson, who was in the top
turret just behind the cockpit, recalls that when they were still a ways
away from Bremen, pilot Fred Delbern tapped him on the shoulder and
told him to look out ahead and said, "We are going to have to fly though
that!" Dodson related what he saw:

> *Ahead of us was a huge black cloud such as I've never seen before
> or since. It was coal black, much darker than any thunder clouds.
> It seemed as if there was no limit to height or length of it. This was
> all coming from the anti-aircraft batteries on the ground.*[2]

The black cloud was from flak-burst smoke from 88-mm antiaircraft batteries on the ground. Bremen was famous for the large number of these guns defending the city, perhaps 250 to one report of eighth hundred as the Germans raced to beef up their bomber defenses. This was very similar to the description of Bremen given by Robert Morgan, pilot of the *Memphis Belle*, several months before.[12]

The implications were obvious. Many airmen have stated that Bremen had the most intense flak than any other target in the Third Reich, even Berlin. Waist gunner Charlie Schreiner said that,

> *Army Intelligence had told us that the Germans had 800 anti-aircraft batteries concentrated in the area and so you can well imagine the rough time the Bombers were having at five miles up. (We felt like clay pigeons).*[36]

The following statement is from tail gunner John Gabay from the Ninety-Fourth Bombardment Group that led the Eighth Army Air Force on this mission to Bremen who confirms the above observations of the crew of the *Polecat*.

> *We were supposed to have plenty of (fighter) escort, but we were late and missed them . . . Flak over the target (Bremen) was extra heavy. The sky was black with flak-burst smoke and I could smell it through my oxygen mask. The noise was cruel and the concussions were murderous. Every ship must have had flak holes we had plenty . . . We were told at interrogation that Bremen put up more flak today than any city up to now.*[11]

Flak consists of ugly steel fragments resulting from the explosion of an 88-mm (3.5-inch) shell. These steel fragments can penetrate an aircraft shell or windshield, causing serious damage to the aircraft and injury or death to the airmen on board. A well-placed flak shell explosion can seriously damage or destroy a B-17 and cause it to explode or simply break apart, which happened on many occasions. After so many months, days, and hours of intensive training, the ten young men on the *Polecat* were in the heart of Germany and face-to-face with the horror of war.

CHAPTER 6

BOMB RUN AND FLAK HITS

1302 to 1310 Hours: Begin Bomb Run

As they began their bomb run approaching Bremen, flak became very intense "of a barrage type," creating a virtual kill zone where hundreds of 88-mm cannons on the ground were firing at the bombers and the *Polecat* was hit several times. Doral Hupp was in the ball turret below the aircraft body and recalls what he saw,

> Just before we hit the target, all hell broke loose. Flak was very heavy and German fighter pilots were everywhere . . . our plane lurched up and down due to being hit by flak and enemy gunfire. A bolt of flak hit the right side of the plane between #3 and #4 engines. It left a hole in the wing large enough to throw a kitchen stove through.[2]

Loren Dodson recalls,

> We began the bomb-run when suddenly there was a terrible jolt; the plane lurched and rolled: this was when we were hit by anti-aircraft fire.[2]

Charlie Schreiner recalls the flak hit was even worse,

> The sky appeared like a piece of cloth with a polka-dot pattern from all the Flak the Germans were throwing up. A few moments

later there was a violent explosion under our aircraft and we went into a violent dive. Darter, Lee, and I were knocked down by concussion and pinned to the floor by centrifugal force of the spinning motion. Delbern and Neff managed to pull the plane out of the dive and when I got back to my position I observed that our former formation of planes was now little specks high above us and that we were now flying alone. Engine #3 was damaged, on fire and throwing oil. The bomb bay doors were torn and buckled. The interphone system had been wrecked, and to add to our danger we had lost approximately 5,000 feet of altitude in enemy territory.[36]

Delbern and Neff finally got the plane leveled out, but the situation was very dangerous at this point as bombardier Ed Woollen "informed him [Delbern] that the bomb bays were afire."[3]

Flak hitting the inside #3 engine on the right side caused a rapid drop in oil pressure and also penetrated the aircraft in many places, injuring several crew members. Pilot Delbern immediately feathered the #3 engine after it was hit—he stopped the engine in a position that the edge of the prop blades is edged on to the air of the moving aircraft and presents the least amount of drag, otherwise a stopped flat prop would cause a large amount of drag. Even worse, a windmilling propeller with an oil-less engine may lead to seized reduction gearing and loss of the propeller, with possible damage to the aircraft. Thereafter, during their interrogation reports that night back at Horham, many other crews would refer to the *Polecat* as the B-17 with the "feathered #3 engine."[4] A stopped engine was a very distinct feature on a flying aircraft (see photo in chapter 5 of a nearly identical B-17F with #2 feathered).

Photo of a 95th BG B-17 over Bremen, Germany, December 16, 1943, flying into a black nightmare of antiaircraft gun flak explosions. (Aircraft 237826 was piloted by Lt. Tucker of the 95th A-Group High Squadron). (Photo credit United States Army Air Corps)

Navigator Pete Jackson, sitting just behind the bombardier Ed Woollen in the very front nose cone of the B-17, had a shocking ringside seat and observed that the flak was terrible going into the bomb run, and the aircraft was badly hit. Doral Hupp in the ball turret felt flak hit the turret, but it did not injure him. However, a lot of flak shrapnel went through the plane and injured several of the crew. Waist gunner Charlie Schreiner was hit in the hand, severing the tendon of his thumb, and was also hit in the kneecap, which he said "hurt like hot coals." He suffered a lot from these wounds for years to come. His thumb was never the same throughout his life.

1310 Hours: Bombs Away

Despite being over a mile below the 95th formation and the entire bomber stream, the *Polecat* pilots Fred and Don could see them clearly above and in front of them. Bombs were dropped by the lead 95th plane and then at 1310 by all aircraft in their group including the *Polecat*. This point was in the center of the flak area, which were the German submarine construction facilities on the River Weser near Bremen. Bombs were dropped by the main 95th A and B formations at 1310 hours from 23,600 feet on the aerial markers dropped by the PFF aircraft flying in the 95th A Group (PFF means pathfinder bombing using the Norden bombsight).[4] The bombs are dropped from all planes at the same time when the lead PFF plane drops. The operations report states that a tight formation was being flown and all bombs were dropped at the same time. Doral Hupp in the ball turret beneath the aircraft said,

> *I saw the multitude of bombs dropped by the squadron, heading for the target at Bremen. It is hard to describe the shapes and sizes of the multitude of those bombs that were falling.*[2]

One or more 88-mm antiaircraft shells (flak) that exploded just beneath the plane (likely under the radio room or further back behind the aircraft center of gravity) not only caused the rapid loss of altitude (by pushing up the tail and lowering the nose) but badly damaged the bomb bay doors. Bombardier Ed Woolen called radioman Eugene Darter on the interphone about the bomb bay doors not opening properly. Loren Dodson recalls,

> *The bomb bay doors were damaged from flak and would not open automatically when Bombardier Ed Woolen pushed the button. Woolen had to literally crawl back between my legs [as Loren was standing manning the top turret] to open the door into the bomb bay and pull the emergency release handle to release the bombs. The bombs pushed through the doors and forced them open and went out of the plane on target.*[2]

After the bombs were dropped through the bomb bay doors, Charlie recalls a problem,

> *At this time, Woollen and Darter were attempting to force open the left bomb bay door as some incendiary bombs, which could not be released from the brackets, were exuding their highly combustible chemicals.*[36]

Then after all bombs were out of the plane, the large bomb bay doors would not close when Woollen threw the switch. This increased drag on the aircraft contributed to their continuing loss of altitude, along with the feathered #3 engine. The *Polecat* was now a mile below the 95th formation and could not keep up and dropped behind and became a "straggler" to the main 95th formation. The original bombing altitude was 23,600 feet at 1310, but by about 1325 they had lost altitude to 18,000 feet as noted by Loren Dodson, the flight engineer.

The following information is from a letter dated May 14, 1946, Headquarters, American Graves Registration Command, European Theater Area, APO 887, US Army. It is based on the 95th crew interrogation reports given back at base that night:

> *Aircraft B-17F, #42-30255 departed on a mission to Bremen, Germany, 16 December 1943. The aircraft is thought to have been hit by anti-aircraft fire just before reaching the target. The #3 engine was lost causing the plane to drop back out of formation. It continued over the target, dropped its bombs, losing altitude and dropping further behind the formation.*[23]

The *Polecat* was in very serious trouble as it came out of the Bremen target and flak area over a mile below and further behind the protection of the formation with severe damage to the aircraft, one engine shot out over 175 miles from home base and with no US fighter escort in sight. And the worst was still to come.

CHAPTER 7

ATTACK BY ENEMY AIRCRAFT JUST AFTER TARGET

1310 to 1325 Hours: Fifteen Minutes of Pure Hell

Almost immediately after the *Polecat* dropped her bombs on the Bremen submarine facilities and came out of the flak area one mile below the formation, the straggling B-17F was attacked by a dozen enemy aircraft. The crew found themselves fighting for their very lives. Can you imagine the shock of the rookie crew about what had just happened over Bremen from the antiaircraft shells hitting the *Polecat* and then suddenly they were under severe attacks from enemy fighters?

Loren Dodson states,

> *The mission had some protection from P-51's (this was one of the first missions with this protection). However, after the bomb run when the enemy aircraft attacked, pilot Fred Delbern called for help and they did not appear. The Lonesome Polecat II was not attacked by enemy aircraft prior to the bomb run.*[2]

As soon as the enemy aircraft were sighted and began their attack, the crew began firing from all positions. The *Polecat* vibrated intensely, and the noise level was extremely high. Bob McKeegan was firing from his tail gun position, Frank Lee and Charlie Schreiner from their waist gun positions, Doral Hupp from his ball turret position on the underside of the aircraft, Loren Dodson in the top turret, Eugene Darter manning the machine gun out of the top radio hatch, and Ed Woollen and Pete Jackson manning the guns in the nose of the plane.

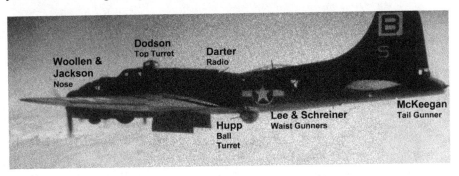

Crew firepower in the B-17. (Photo credit United States Army Air Corps, *Polecat* crew names added by M. I. Darter)

This was a lot of firepower (they had 7,000 rounds onboard), but they needed all of it to survive the many attacking enemy aircraft. Each of the crew saw the battle from their own position.

Loren Dodson recalls what he experienced in the top turret position,

> *When we came off the target and fell behind and below the formation, two ME109's came in on us out of the sun. We knocked down the first one, but the second one kept on coming and it looked like he would ram the plane before we were able to blow it up. He got in close enough that he shot out the inboard engine on the left wing (#2 engine) and started a fire in the engine and wing. Wreckage from his plane floated across the wings of our plane.[2]*

The diagram[4] on the next page shows just one of the numerous combat report diagrams, this one showing the B Group with an enemy aircraft coming in on their tail and was hit and exploded. This one may be the fighter that Loren describes above. Loren continues,

> *After this the attacks began coming from the tail. This one ME109 was making a pass at us. I was firing at him and he at us when he hit the dome of my turret with a 20-mm shell. He blew a hole in*

the dome of the turret; pieces of shrapnel and Plexiglas hitting me in the face and knocking me out of the turret. I landed just back of the pilot's and copilot's seats, my face was bleeding and I was dazed. I lay on the floor for a few moments and I reached up and touched Delbern on the arm. He turned to see what I wanted and saw what had happened. He told me to get my chute on and get out of the plane. He also said that Pete Jackson and Eddie Woollen had already left the plane.[2]

Hupp remembers Dodson getting hit in the top turret and hearing him scream. Dodson was hit by flying shrapnel in the face, which caused him a lot of bleeding, but fortunately, it was not mortal.

A written statement by Doral Hupp (written on the back of the form after his release from POW in 1945) stated,

After crossing target, formation left us. Fighter attacks from front and rear and both sides, approx. 12 planes. Attack lasted from 15 to 30 minutes. Damage done by attack was as follows: all men wounded except tail gunner (McKeegan) and myself, radio operator (Darter) seriously in arm. The plane was badly shattered by flak and fighters. No. 2 engine afire and inter-phone shot out. Five enemy planes shot down. Bombardier (Woollen), navigator (Jackson) and engineer (Dodson) bailed near Oldenburg, Germany.[2]

Ed Woollen in the nose bombardier position related to his son, John Woollen, the following:

After completing their bomb run, their ship was attacked by numerous enemy fighters. During one attack, he was badly wounded in the abdomen by machine gun or cannon fire from one of the attacking German fighters when a bullet entered his back just above right kidney. He had a round, quarter-sized scar on his back in this area. He believed he would have been killed outright, except that the bullet must have spent most of its energy before striking him due to either long range or because it passed through part of the aircraft before hitting him.[24]

Charlie Schreiner, writing in November 1945, provides the most detailed recollection of this tragic fifteen-minute period without fighter protection:

> *The first Nazi attack came from the front and Eddie Woollen managed to knock down one of the bastards. Eddie's position was riddled by machine gun bullets. Loren Dodson in the top turret was knocked out cold by a 20-mm that exploded near his face. A week later I met him in prison. He had two beautiful black eyes and was pretty well scratched up. Also in this encounter #2 engine was damaged and on fire.*
>
> *The second attack came from the rear at McKeegan's position. Doral, Lee and I heard Mac's guns open up and we all swung our guns toward the tail to give him our support and cover. In this pass Darter, Lee, and I were knocked off our feet by exploding enemy machine-gun fire. Darter was down for keeps.*
>
> *Together, Lee and I crawled back to our guns. A portion of my window was blasted out, my ammunition box riddled and shattered, and my ammunition carrier splintered in jagged edges. I felt a sharp, steady pain in my arm and leg and noticed that my left shoe and glove felt wet. This was my first knowledge that I had been hit. Both Lee and I were bleeding profusely from the nose and mouth. but at the time I figured it must have been the effects of concussion. In an attempt to get my gun in firing order for the next Nazi charge, I discovered my left hand was paralyzed. Lee sensed the situation and braced my weapon while I tried to snap a round into the lips of my damaged 50 Caliber. I could still pull a trigger and was ready for the next attack.*
>
> *Meanwhile, the enemy fighters had made a wide circle to the rear. This time for the Kill!*
>
> *All the guns on the plane were chattering and we felt the impact of enemy bullets hitting our ship. McKeegan knocked two of the bastards down, I got one, and Doral got a probable.*[36]

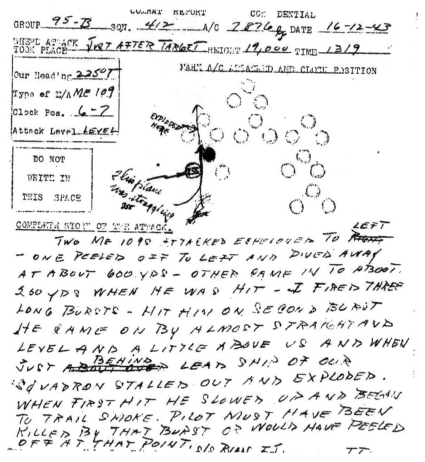

One of the several combat reports for the 95th BG for the December 16, 1943, mission to Bremen, Germany. This enemy fighter shot out the *Polecat #2* engine. Note the handwritten comment, "This plane was straggling." This was the original position of the *Lonesome Polecat II* (#230255).[4]
(Image credit United States Army Air Corps)

Charlie told me that he saw my brother standing, shooting his 50-caliber machine gun out the radio room top hatch, when he was hit by incoming enemy aircraft fire. He fell on the floor of the plane on his back, bleeding profusely. He could not help Eugene for a time because the fighting was furious with many fighter attacks. They were fighting for their lives. Charlie hit and shot down several fighters but was hit in the wrist and kneecap by flak during the bomb run. The wrist wound severed the tendon of his thumb, which did not work throughout his life. His knee was the most painful, "like a red-hot poker," he said. He saw holes all over the plane from flak and bullets. They sounded like hail hitting the plane. Different groups of fighters came up during the fighter attack to shoot at them.[2]

Charlie also stated the following regarding the tail gunner Bob McKeegan:

Later I learned that Mac had one of his guns shot out of his hands and that he was holding his position with a single gun.[36]

Nightmare in the Cockpit

In the cockpit during this fifteen-minute period of fierce fighter attacks, the rookie pilots Fred Delbern and Don Neff were living a nightmare. They were a mile below the protection of the formation, the #3 engine was lost, their aircraft was badly damaged by flak over Bremen, and now they were a straggler which immediately attracted numerous enemy aircraft who began aggressively attacking in all directions. Numerous cannon shells had hit the *Polecat*, and black smoke was now pouring out of the #2 engine. Pilot Fred Delbern suddenly realized they could not escape from this horror and ordered a bailout. The three up-front crew (Ed, Pete, and Loren after he was blasted out of the top turret) heard the order and left the stricken B-17F. The five men in the rear of the plane were still shooting at attacking fighters and the noise intensity and focus was such that no one heard the bailout order.

At this moment, about 1325 hours, just after Loren bailed out near Leer, Germany (Loren told me that the pilots were not hit before he bailed), another frontal enemy attack blasted the cockpit and the two pilots. Fred was hit in the left arm by shrapnel and was bleeding, and smoke blackened his face. Sadly, Don was hit more severely from a cannon shell through or near the windshield and immediately slumped over in his copilot's seat, unable to fly the aircraft. Fred was stunned as he tried to comprehend what just happened to his friend and able copilot Don Neff. But somehow through this nightmare, he was able to focus on survival, keeping the *Polecat* in the air but losing altitude, heading westward following the bomber stream high above them toward the turning point, a Dutch island called Texel.

1325 Hours: Suddenly, It Was Quiet

Then just after 1325 hours, when the *Polecat* had become extremely vulnerable with the navigator, bombardier, and top turret gunner gone and the copilot fatally wounded, the attackers vanished. The guns in the rear of the aircraft grew quiet. Fred scanned the sky through the cockpit windows but saw no enemy fighters. Since he had ordered a bailout several minutes prior and the guns were quiet in the rear of the plane, he assumed that all crew had left the *Polecat*.

The enemy fighters suddenly disappeared, and amazingly, there were no further attacks on the straggling *Polecat* as it continued losing altitude, with the #2 engine trailing thick black smoke and the #3 feathered, but heading directly west toward the Dutch coast and the Texel Island turning point toward England. Fred was following the bomber stream specks now more than two miles above him.

But high above, an ace German pilot was watching the straggling bomber, just waiting for the American escort to depart and dive down and destroy the straggling B17.

95th Groups A and B Crew Interrogation Reports Related to the Polecat

The crews that survived the mission were interrogated upon return to the 95th base at Horham, England. The following was excerpted from the 95th operational records for the December 16, 1943, mission that are related to the low squadron that included the *Polecat* (the pilots' names are listed first): [4]

- *Casper crew reported: Attack on low squadron after leaving target 10 minutes. Two attacked from 1 and 2 o'clock. An attack from side. B-17 out of 95B—13:25—#2 engine smoking. 4 chutes*
- *Conley crew reported: ME 109 and FW190 from top point over formation then attack from 6 o'clock low in pairs.*
  One B-17 just after target 13:14 seen out of formation. 1 chute seen although plane seemed to follow us back. (Note: This was the *Polecat*, and the plane "seemed to follow us back" means that the Conley crew saw the bomber trying to maintain the

flight path back to England behind and way below the main formation that eventually took them over Texel Island off the coast of Holland.)

- *Dean crew reported: The attacks were from high to low level on the low squadron. After the stragglers. The last 3 ships (enemy aircraft) then would peel off and come around and attack from the rear.*
  One chute seen out of B-17 or E/A at 13:20. This B-17 was a "straggler" #3 engine feathered. This B-17 goes on, E/A (enemy aircraft) destroyed (not one already noted).
- *Hamby crew reported: FW 190 and ME 109 aggressive on formation below.*
- *Rogers crew reported: 5 attacks on tail; from target to 52-52'N-07-10'E. Duration 22 minutes. Very aggressive at 21,000 ft.*
- *McCallister crew reported: 3 men bailed out of B-17 from group behind.*
- *Hubbs crew reported: 5 E/A attacked low squadron from 6 o'clock. 2 turned away and then were shot down.*
- *Hubbs crew reported: 13:19 hours, 3 chutes bail out of B-17 far below us at 4 o'clock. We were 22,100 ft. altitude. E/A made 3 passes at B-17. It was not on fire.*
- *Infield crew reported: 1 B-17 at 13:25 (group low and behind us)—seemed to be ok but 3 chutes came out.*
- *Leonard crew reported: Saw B-17 hit by fighter just after target (4 min). 3 chutes out but B-17 continued under control and fighters left him alone.*
- *Wallace crew reported: About 13:15 E/A hit by our other group burst into flames and went down just behind that formation.*
  Saw 2 chutes from 2 B-17's at 13:25 and 13:35. These were stragglers under attack by E/A. Don't know what group (Note: they were likely from the *Polecat* as no one bailed out of any other 95th aircraft).
- *Brink Crew reported: 13:20 A B-17 seen in fight with 2 enemy aircraft.*

The last official sighting of the *Polecat* was stated as follows in a letter dated May 14, 1946, Headquarters, American Graves Registration

Command, European Theater Area, APO 887, US Army, based on the evening interrogation reports:

> *Aircraft B-17F, #42-30255 departed on a mission to Bremen, Germany, 16 December 1943. The aircraft is thought to have been hit by anti-aircraft fire just before reaching the target. The #3 engine was lost causing the plane to drop back out of formation. It continued over the target, dropped its bombs, losing altitude and dropping further behind the formation. Fighters were then seen to attack the B-17 and three chutes were reported. The aircraft continued losing altitude but seemed otherwise under control until it disappeared in the clouds about 53 degrees 05' E" (29 miles west of Bremen).*[23]

The *Polecat* was officially considered to be lost to both flak and fighters based on the interrogation reports.

Why Didn't the Enemy Aircraft Finish off the Polecat? Just-in-time Miracle!

From bombs away at 1310 to about 1325 hours, the crippled aircraft was straggling behind and below the 95th formation under full-scale attack from enemy fighters. Charlie Schreiner observed that the enemy fighters made a wide circle to the rear, "This time for the kill!" But the kill never came. Why? Both Doral and Charlie told me they were very surprised that the enemy aircraft did not finish them off after the fierce aerial attacks. Why not?

The answer to this mystery was discovered when reading the operational record of the 95th Bomb Group for December 16, 1943.[4] This document states that the US fighter escorts finally located the bombers at 1325 (the weather had hindered the location of the bombers by the fighters prior to this). This is the precise moment when the enemy aircraft would have surely finished off the very vulnerable *Polecat* had not the US fighter escort (which included one of the first missions of the famous P-51 Mustangs) showed up and saved them from certain death. Thank God for the American escorts! Now what is next?

CHAPTER 8

"BAIL OUT, WE CANNOT MAKE IT BACK!"

1320 to 1325 Hours: Bailout of Three Airmen

Several returning crews of the 95th BG stated that three chutes came out of the B-17 "with the feathered #3 engine" toward the end of the enemy fighter attack. Lt. Ed Woollen, the bombardier, "informed him [Delbern] that the bomb bays were afire and agreed with him to give order to bail out."[3] Lt. Fred Delbern ordered a bail out at that critical time because he did not believe that they could make it back given the extent of flak and fighter damage and the continuing onslaught of fighter attacks. Royal "Pete" Jackson (the navigator) recalls Lt. Delbern ringing the bailout bell[2], and he was the first to bail out. Pete was immediately followed by Ed, and they came down near Oldenburg, Germany. After a few minutes, Loren Dodson (engineer and top turret gunner) was hit in the top turret, collapsed on the floor, and then ordered by Delbern to bail out immediately. He landed beyond Oldenburg near Leer, Germany.

Loren Dodson Recollections

Dodson's face was badly bloodied after the attacking ME109 hit his turret with a 20-mm shell and shattered it, causing pieces of shrapnel and Plexiglas to hit his face. This knocked him dazed onto the floor of the aircraft just behind the cockpit. He reached up and touched pilot Fred Delbern on the arm and was told to get on a chute and get out of the aircraft because they "cannot make it back." He also said that Pete Jackson and Eddie Woollen had already left the plane. Dodson quickly observed that the altimeter indicated 18,000 feet, which was over a mile below their original bombing altitude of nearly 24,000 feet but still far above the clouds that covered the ground below.

The escape procedure was for me to jump from the bomb bay. I got my chute on and took a couple of looks out the bomb bay. All I could see below me was clouds and they looked like they were a thousand miles away. I just couldn't do it, so I went into the bombardier-navigator compartment to an escape hatch where Eddie and Pete had bailed out. I sat down on the catwalk, stuck my feet out the hatch and lowered myself down until the slipstream caught me and pulled me out of the plane.

I tumbled and rolled before I opened my chute. We were using the 24-foot canopy type chutes and when that opened it looked about the size of an umbrella. I wondered what in the world they had done to me. We were told to watch our chutes; the air-currants could roll the sides in and if they went too far the chute could collapse. The sides were rolling in but I didn't know just how far they had to go before it would collapse. The up-drafts would hit the chute and there were times when you felt as if you were going back up again.

I spoke about tumbling and rolling when I jumped. I had on a pair of sheepskin flying boots. You took off your shoes to put them on, so before I jumped I tied the shoes laces together and hung them around my neck. When I reached the ground my shoes were gone as well as one of the boots. I had a new pocket knife that dad had given me when I was home on furlough and that was gone also.

I broke through the clouds; they were so low I just had time to catch a glimpse of a farm family standing in their backyard. I remember hitting the ground and going down on one knee. When I came to I was lying on my back and his family was gathered around me. They had unbuckled my chute hairiness and removed my oxygen mask and helmet. An old German man said in rough English, "For you, the war is over." They wanted to know if I had a gun and they helped me up and took me in the house and gave me a chair near the fire-place and brought me a cup of their coffee; tasted pretty good! The farmer gave me a lecture on FDR, the S.O.B. as he referred to him. He called the authorities and they came and took me to an army base at Leer, Germany and put me in a hospital where I spent the night after they had dressed the wounds in my face and given me a tetanus shot.[2]

Dodson was captured on December 16, 1943, at 1400 hours in Burlage, District Leer. He had blood all over him and two very black eyes and could not open his jaw to eat. Several days later, he was interrogated by a German officer, who was very friendly, offered him a cigarette, and, after he refused to say anything but his name, rank, and serial number, opened a book and proceeded to tell him virtually everything about his training. He told Dodson where he was trained, the dates, the other crew members, bases, etc. They appeared to know everything about him, which came as a great shock to Loren (note: Doral Hupp had the same experience).

The officer told the astonished Dodson that his plane (the *Lonesome Polecat II*) had crashed into the North Sea. As stated, Dodson noted the altimeter was at eighteen-thousand-foot elevation when he bailed out. Since the bomb run was at 23,600 feet, the plane had lost over a mile of altitude when the flak shell went off beneath the aircraft. The first engine to be shot out by flak on the bomb run was the right innermost engine (#3). Then the enemy aircraft knocked out the right inner engine (#2), which was smoking and on fire. In addition, as Doral Hupp and Loren Dodson stated, the bomb bay doors were still dangling open, causing drag on the aircraft, and a large hole in the right wing resulted in loss of lift. Pilots Delbern and Neff clearly had to struggle to keep the plane airborne in this condition as it continued to lose altitude.

Royal (Pete) Jackson Recollections

Royal (Pete) Jackson wrote that when he heard the bailout bell, he went up to the cockpit from his navigator position in the nose cone to talk to the pilot and copilot. He and copilot Don Neff were good friends, and Jackson said to Neff, who was in the copilot's seat, "Come on, Don, let's get out of here." Pilot Fred Delbern said, "No, Don, you're needed here." Jackson further wrote that he saw the first pilot and copilot before jumping, both in their flying positions, with the copilot flying and first pilot holding one arm with the other hand as if injured. Neff gave him "a wave of the hand and a smile." Jackson told me that he did not believe Neff was injured at that time.[3] Pilot Delbern gave Jackson a smile and a nod of the head, and Jackson went back down to the front of the aircraft and put on his parachute and prepared to bail out.

As he jumped out the assigned door in the left front of the aircraft near his navigation station, he was hit in the eye with an exploding flak particle. This almost put him into shock as he fell through the air and caused lots of loss of blood that was all over his clothes and skin. This was so painful and shocking that Jackson told me he does not remember pulling his chute chord, coming down, or hitting the ground. The fact that he actually pulled his chute pin was in itself a miracle and of course saved his life. He was captured near Oldenburg, Germany, and was placed in a German hospital for a few months and remembers spending Christmas in the hospital. Although his eye was treated in a German hospital and later in the US, he was not able to see from it again.[2]

Junius (Ed) Woollen Recollections

Lt. Ed Woollen bailed out just after Jackson. Woollen reported that he "informed him [Delbern] that the bomb bays were afire and agreed with him to give order to bail out." He stated that Delbern was injured, "Hit in arm, leg, and abdomen," but that he was in his seat trying to control the plane.[3] John Woollen, son of Ed Woollen (note that Woollen had gone on two prior missions as a fill-in with another crew), reports the following recollection of his father's experience:

> His plane was shot down on his third combat mission, which took place very soon after he arrived in England. During the mission, the German anti-aircraft artillery was very heavy, and his aircraft was hit by heavy flak on the way to the target. Apparently everyone in the crew was wounded by flak to varying extents. He said his flak wounds were "not bad." (However, I recall that up until his death, he periodically would go to the local Air Force hospital to have pieces of shrapnel surgically removed that had, as he put it, "Worked its way out.")

After completing their bomb run, their ship was attacked by numerous enemy fighters. During one attack, he was badly wounded in the abdomen by machine gun or cannon fire from one of attacking German fighters when a bullet entered his back just above right kidney. (He had a round, quarter-sized scar on his back in this area). He believed he would have been killed outright, except that the bullet must have spent most of its energy before striking him due to either long range or because it passed through part of the aircraft before hitting him.

He was bleeding profusely, and bailed out while he was close to losing consciousness. Dad believed that if he had not bailed out, he would not have made it back to his base before he bled to death.

When he reached the ground after parachuting from the plane, he was captured immediately by German troops. He said that the German doctor who sewed him up and stopped the bleeding "saved his life" (Woollen landed near Oldenburg, Germany).[24]

Robert McKeegan Recollections

Tail gunner Bob McKeegan wrote in 1945 that Lt. Neff and Lt. Delbern "stayed at the controls trying to get the ship back to England and just didn't make it. Two props were windmilling, and #2 engine was on fire."[3]

Meanwhile, in the Back of the Polecat

Amazingly, the five crew members in the back of the plane did not know that the three men up front had bailed out. With the exception of the ball turret, the intercom system was completely out to the back of the plane. Pete Jackson told me specifically that Delbern pulled the bailout bell and must have thought all crew had left the aircraft. The bell signal was supposed to consist of three short rings on the alarm bell. At first alarm, all crew members put on parachutes. Then the signal to abandon ship was one long ring on alarm bell. However, none of the men in the back of the aircraft heard any bailout signals as they were under intense attack from enemy aircraft and the noise levels from firing their machine guns was very high to say nothing of their total focus on survival.

The pilot could not readily see the men in the back of the aircraft because there are two sets of doors between the cockpit and the rear of the aircraft that were closed. Another reason for lack of communication appears to be related to the injuries of the pilot, the intense struggle to keep the damaged aircraft under control, and the damage to the interphone. Evidence indicates that copilot Don Neff was fatally wounded and pilot Fred Delbern wounded in his arm and totally consumed with keeping the aircraft airborne. It must also be remembered that this was the very first combat mission for this crew, and no amount of training can prepare one for the severe trauma that they experienced thus far on the mission.

CHAPTER 9

RETURN OF THE 95TH BOMBARDMENT GROUP TO ENGLAND

After bombs away at 1310, the main 95th BG (A and B formations) continued on the planned flight path which crossed over Texel Island (the Netherlands). They crossed Texel at 1358 (A Group) and 1359 (B Group).[4] The flight from Bremen to Texel Island had taken fifty minutes in total. About fifteen minutes of this time, immediately after bombs away, involved the attacks by many enemy aircraft that ended only when the US fighter escort located the bombers and drove them off.

Note that the average ground speed of the main 95th BG formation was approximately 203 mph, as calculated by dividing the distance from Bremen to Texel Island (166 miles) by the flight time (1310 to 1359). The English coast was reached by the 95th BG after another thirty-five minutes at 1434 hours just north of Lowestoft as shown below. Note that the direction from Bremen to Texel is exactly due west parallel to and just above the fifty-third parallel.[4]

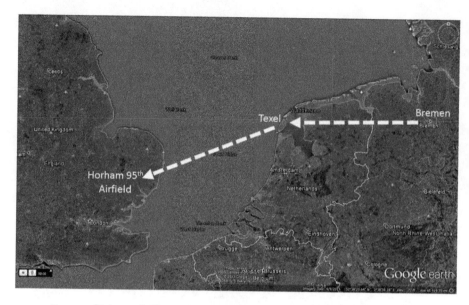

Return flight path from Bremen to England on December 16, 1943
(Image credit Google Earth)

Upon landing, the returning 95th BG crews each went through interrogation to feedback from the crew on many details pertaining to the mission. The 95th BG staff then prepared a detailed operations report that included many facts about the mission, including observations of enemy aircraft attacking the bombers, anti-aircraft flak attacks from the ground, bombing accuracy, parachutes out of aircraft, claims of shoot downs of enemy aircraft, and of course sightings of their own aircraft being hit or with engine problems and lost or missing aircraft. The 95th BG operations report for December 16, 1943, Bremen has over 150 pages of detailed information, and the original is available at the National Archives. I never will forget the experience of requesting the operations report for that day and when it was delivered to my table at the National Archives II, going through it page by page, wondering if I was the first one to see these original documents since 1943. Of course, other researchers had probably handled the many loose pages all hand typed or handwritten by 95th BG operations personnel the night of and the day after the mission was completed. While several B-17s were hit badly, the *Polecat* was the only one that was missing on this mission from the 95th BG. The following is one of the summaries found in the report related to the *Polecat*:

Aircraft 230255 is missing. It was seen to leave the formation with #3 engine out just before target but continued on to drop bombs on target and then fell back. Enemy aircraft attacked this ship west of target and three chutes came out. Aircraft was last seen 10 minutes from target disappearing into clouds but still under control.

When I first read this in the beginning of the investigation, my mind immediately wondered, "Three chutes came out. Aircraft was last seen ten minutes from target, disappearing into clouds but still under control." Was my brother one of those three chutes, so he would have landed near Oldenburg? Or was he still on the Flying Fortress? If so, why didn't he bail out? Was he wounded or worse? And of course, what happened to the damaged aircraft and the remaining crew? This story is far from over.

CHAPTER 10

RETURN FLIGHT OF THE STRICKEN AND STRAGGLING *POLECAT*

After Pete Jackson and Ed Woollen bailed out near Oldenburg and Loren Dodson bailed out near Leer, Germany, the *Lonesome Polecat II* was seen to disappear into clouds but was noted to be "under control" in spite of losing #2 (on fire) and #3 engines. The bomb bay doors were still dangling open, and a large hole in the wing existed, all causing additional drag on the aircraft. In addition, the top turret was blasted and inoperable, and Bob McKeegan in the tail had one of his twin guns shot out of his hands.[36] This was the last time that the plane was identified in the interrogation reports by other crews. The Missing Aircraft Crew Report (MACR) 1558[3] includes an *X* at this point on a map of Europe as the aircraft's last known location, which is approximately twenty-nine miles west of Bremen.

Pilot Lt. Fred Delbern initially thought that with all the aircraft damage and continuing enemy aircraft attacks, they could not get back to England when he ordered the bailout. He specifically ordered the three men up front to bail out in person and knew that they had bailed (as Loren related). However, miraculously, just as the enemy fighters were about to make their kill of the *Polecat*, the US fighter escort of P-51s and P-47s arrived at 1325, and the enemy fighters disappeared. Talk about a miracle for saving the seven crew members still on board. And the severely damaged Flying Fortress was still flying and had not blown up as so many B-17s.

1325 to 1450 Hours: Polecat Flight to Dutch Coast

Lt. Fred Delbern, apparently thinking that all of the crew had left the aircraft except copilot Neff and himself, continued on heading due west, losing altitude toward England. He followed the miles-long bomber stream that he could see through the windshield high above him. They were now well behind and perhaps more than ten thousand feet below the main 95th BG formation and continuing to lose altitude. The *Polecat* was observed by other crews to be a "straggler" and to "follow them back" in the distance. Delbern, having been injured in the arm and perhaps more, struggled greatly to keep the aircraft airborne with only two working engines, and fortunately they were the two outboard engines #1 and #4.

But the *Polecat* had experienced this situation before, November 13, in fact, also flying back from Bremen. Two engines were shot out, holes all over the aircraft, two men dead on board, with very experienced Lt. John Miller in control (see chapter 5 for this story), who somehow brought the *Polecat* back to their Horham base.

Lt. Delbern also kept the *Polecat* directly on the planned 95th BG westerly flight path even though there was total cloud cover below them. He likely was following the direction of the bomber stream overhead. But as Delbern approached the Dutch coast, he was faced with the most important decision of his life: what to do next? Could the *Polecat* make it back all the way over the North Sea to England without exploding (it was still a long distance back to England), or should he bailout over land, or should he ditch the aircraft near the coast? This decision would result in the life or death of the pilots and anyone remaining on board.

During this time, only the two waist gunners realized that radioman Eugene Darter was critically wounded with a shattered arm and lay bleeding on the floor of the radio room. During this time, there was continuous heavy undercast covering the ground, and the crew in the back of the plane could not tell if they were over land or water.

The *Polecat* flew on for approximately twenty-five minutes after the attacks stopped (1325 hours) until they reached the Dutch coast. The 95th BG A and B formations were several minutes ahead of them, traveling faster (about 203 mph ground speed) with all engines working and at a higher altitude. The *Polecat* with only two engines had lost a lot of altitude and was now well below 10,000 feet as they approached the Dutch coastline.

Doral A. Hupp's observation,

> *After the bombing run on Bremen, it is my recollection that we lost altitude after the plane suffered heavy damage from flak and enemy-aircraft fire. This attack lasted 10 to 20 minutes, by my recollection. We went down enough that we were able to go off oxygen. We also had Allied fighter escort at that time._We encountered no additional enemy aircraft or flak from this time until we bailed out over Texel Island.[2]*

Note Hupp's statement that they had fighter escort during this time. This explains why no further attacks were made on the *Polecat* after the rendezvous at 1325 hours with the fighter escort.

Hupp (who was in the ball turret) also stated that after they had flown on for a while, a German observation plane surprisingly came up directly under the B-17, and for a few seconds, he and the pilot stared at each other. He instinctively blasted the enemy aircraft out of the sky. To this day, Hupp has no idea why the observation plane flew so dangerously close to the *Polecat* other than the enemy observation plane may have thought the crew had bailed out and the plane was on autopilot.

German Fighters Following Lonesome Polecat Overhead

Unseen to Fred or the other crew on board, there were now two German fighter aircraft high above them following and watching the B-17F straggler trying to escape to the coast. One of the pilots was a top German ace with many kills. Had there not been the US fighter escort, they would have no doubt swooped down and blasted the *Polecat* out of the sky, killing all seven crew still on board. More about these two pilots in chapter 14.[37]

Graphic of Return Flight

The following graphic was prepared to give the distances, times, and events that occurred along the way from "bombs away" over the target (Bremen) until the *Polecat* passed over Texel Island. Note that altitude is shown on the vertical axis and distance and time on the horizontal axis.

This one illustration shows time, distance, and the specific events of the mission taking place.

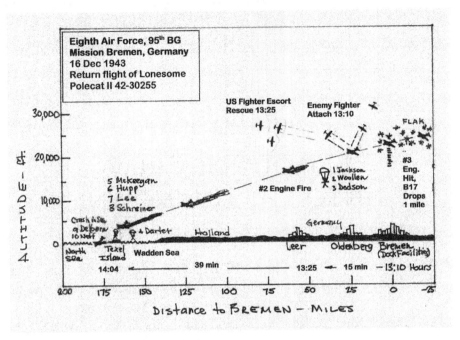

Events that occurred to the *Polecat* B-17F from its bombing run prior to the target (Bremen) until it crashed into the North Sea (based on all available information) (Image credit M. I. Darter)

CHAPTER 11

BAILOUT OF CREW
INTO THE UNKNOWN

The westerly flight path of the 95th BG and the straggling *Polecat* following far behind and below is shown on the map. The return flight path directed them to fly over a Dutch island called Texel (largest of the Frisian Islands) about twenty-five miles from the Dutch mainland on the flight path out across a shallow body of water called the Wadden Sea. As the severely damaged *Polecat* approached the mainland coast of the Netherlands and then out over the Wadden Sea, the men in the back of the plane did not have any idea where they were as thick clouds and fog covered the entire surface. As time went on, they began to believe that they were over the freezing North Sea.

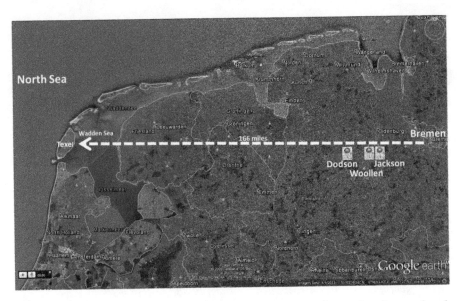

Westward flight path of the *Polecat* following the main formation far overhead
(Image credit Google Earth)

1350 to 1400 Hours: Crossing the Wadden Sea

As the *Polecat* approached the Dutch coast at 1350 hours at just over six-thousand-foot altitude, pilot Lt. Fred Delbern was desperately trying to decide what to do. Should he continue on and try to make it back across the North Sea to their base in Horham, England? This would have required more than fifty minutes of flying at their reduced speed and be able to maintain altitude. No doubt, his own injuries, the fatally injured copilot Don Neff slumped next to him, the continual loss of altitude, the feathered #3 engine, the dangerously smoking and burning #2 engine which could explode at any moment, and Delbern's aversion to bailing out all weighed heavily on him. Unknown to Fred, the five crew members in the back of the *Polecat* did not hear any bailout order and were still manning their guns. Fred desperately needed to assess the condition of the aircraft and tried reaching someone on the intercom. The only working line was to Doral Hupp in the ball turret, who relates the story,

> *Due to enemy fire, the plane's intercom was broken between the pilot and the rear of the plane, except for the ball-turret connection. I could talk to the pilot and he asked me to exit the*

ball-turret and check on the rear of the plane and check the bomb
bay doors. I never got a chance to check the bomb bay doors.[2]

On his way to check the bomb bay doors which were closed off by the door of the radio room, Doral discovered his friend Eugene lying in a pool of blood in the radio room.

Regarding Eugene Darter (radio operator), I first saw Eugene on the floor of the radio room bleeding extensively from the leg and right arm. It was evident that he had been seriously injured as there was a lot of blood strewn all over the radio room and his right arm was bleeding quite a lot. He was lying on his back and did not have his oxygen mask on but he was conscious. I then administered first aid and I gave him a shot of sulphr-melinyde on wound. This was a painkiller that would also help to perk him up, which it did. I also put a tourniquet on his right arm, above the elbow to help stop the bleeding. After that, Eugene stood up and I helped put on his parachute. At this time he appeared to feel very lively and well.

While bandaging Eugene, the pilot, Pilot Fred Delbern appeared outside the cockpit and I spoke very briefly with him regarding the co-pilot and Eugene. He said something like forget about the co-pilot (note: this indicated to Doral that Don Neff was fatally injured). The pilot went back up front after a few moments talking to me. His face black tinted as if there had been a fire up front. That was the only time that he appeared to the rear of the plane. He closed the door between the bomb bay and the pilot section of the plane.[2]

Charlie Schreiner, a waist gunner stationed just behind the radio room, told me that he had seen my brother Eugene hit in the right arm as he was shooting his machine gun out the top hatch of the radio room at an attacking enemy fighter. The radio room was shattered by 20-mm shells, and Darter collapsed on the floor of the radio room with blood streaming out. Schreiner helped Doral Hupp get Darter fixed up as much as he could, but Schreiner was hit by shrapnel and could not use his left arm or hand. He recalled that Hupp put a tourniquet on Darter's arm to stop the bleeding.

Schreiner wrote the following details in November 1945 about what happened just before the bailout:

Delbern had been hit in the left arm and he eventually crawled back through the cat-walk to the radio room to see how we were making out. Our inter-phone system had been knocked out of commission way back at the target so I guess he didn't know exactly what was going on in the rear.

Delbern sized up the situation and orally gave Doral the order that "The Ship was to be Abandoned Immediately." The engine fires were melting the metal off the wings and the plane was vibrating violently from the wind milling prop on #2 engine. Even if the plane had not disintegrated apart in the air from the vibrations, our gas had run so low that we couldn't get halfway over the channel with two engines. Delbern had told Woollen, Jackson, and Dodson to "Abandon All" previously and they had left the ship 10 or 15 minutes before although at the time us fellows in the rear had no knowledge of it.

After Delbern's order, within a few minutes we were prepared to "Bail Out." Darter was weak and his face was white from loss of blood. Doral was helping him and had placed a chute on his chest and had attached a dingy to the rear of his harness. In the meantime, Lee was violently kicking at the warped escape hatch. When the door finally broke off, Lee threw a 50 caliper shell at McKeegan warning him to come out of the tail. Later I learned that Mac had had one of his guns shot out of his hands and that he was holding his position with a single gun.[36]

1400 Hours: Bailout over the Ocean and Die or Stay in the Aircraft until It Explodes and Die

Doral Hupp continues the dramatic story,

Because Eugene's right arm was so badly wounded (it was limber from the wound), I felt that he would be unable to pull the parachute cord with his right arm, so I put his parachute on upside-down so that he could pull the cord with his left arm. Eugene put on his life-vest in the event that he hit the water. He also took his emergency bag with him, which he had prepared before take-off. This bag included some medicines, food, and some tape for emergencies. I told Eugene to wait and jump with me as soon as I got my parachute and my Mae West on.

I noticed that Eugene Darter had gone to the back and was going to bail out. He looked at me and said, "Doral you remember what we talked about?" I said yes (that if this war continued we could all be hurt or worse). He smiled and said, "I'll be all right." Then he jumped out of the plane. I watched him as he opened his chute with his left hand and it worked! Watching him descend down toward the overcast below us, I felt he would be all right, not knowing that we were still over the water. We did not know where we were at that moment.

After aiding Darter, I walked to the back of the plane where Frank Lee and Charles Schreiner were looking out the side windows (also Robert McKeegan had come up from his tail gunner position). Just after Eugene jumped out, a P-47 fighter came up on the left side of us and I waved to him and he tipped his wings in reply and flew off. At that time I saw the #2 engine on fire and smoke was flowing all the way along the left side. I asked Lee how long it had been burning and he said a long time.

At that moment I told them that we all had to bail out of the plane, and for them all to get their chutes and Mae West life jackets on, which they did. This was about five minutes after I had first started to work on Eugene's injuries.

We jumped out of the plane 3 or 4 minutes after Eugene, after we had all our gear on. We all jumped from the back door, right side. Bob McKeegan was the first of us out, with the help of my boot (Bob McKeegan had frozen in the aircraft doorway and Doral had to literally push him out). I went out next followed by Frank Lee and then Charlie Schreiner. We never heard from the pilot regarding the exodus from the plane due to the intercom failure.[2]

After McKeegan, Hupp, and Lee had bailed, Charlie Schreiner was the last one remaining in the back of the aircraft and he told me he seriously thought about which alternative would prolong his life the longest: bailout and die in the ocean or stay on the burning aircraft and die when it exploded and crashed? His recollections of the events are as follows:

> *Of the crew members from the aft of the ship, Darter was the first to leave and his parachute blossomed perfectly. McKeegan, Hupp, and Lee followed in respective order a few minutes later after we had checked parachute harnesses and dinghies. I followed in short order and waved to Lee after my chute had opened.*[36]

Charlie expected to land in the ocean as they could not see the ground due to cloud cover. He said that he had a raft attached so that if he came down in the water, he might survive. After leaving the plane, he experienced "deafening silence" as he floated through the thick clouds to an unknown landing.

Winter Weather Conditions on Texel Island

The weather on that day December 16, 1943, was very cold, with the temperature ranging from a minimum of -2 °C and a maximum of 2.7 °C (28 to 37 °F). It was very misty, and the wind was high between 15 and 25 mph. The North Sea would have been very cold and the waves very large indeed.

Life or Death, a Thin Line

The painting below of the damaged *Lonesome Polecat II* with the remaining crew bailing out over Texel Island was done by John Blott, an artist in Horham, England (the original is displayed in the Red Feather Club at Horham, England). Note the wide-open bomb bay doors, the stopped feathered #3 engine, the fire in #2, and the hole in the wing. As the men's parachutes opened and they silently entered the thick clouds and fog just below them, they thought for sure that they would land in the cold ocean and of course could not last more than a few minutes before hypothermia took over. They were in for the surprise of their lives.

Stricken *Lonesome Polecat II* over Texel Island with crew bailing
out December 16, 1943 (Image credit artist John Blott, Horham, UK)

CHAPTER 12

AS WOUNDED S/SGT. DARTER CAME THROUGH THE THICK UNDERCAST

Eugene Darter was born January 3, 1913, in Long Beach, California, where he grew up and graduated from LB Polytechnic High School and on to four years of college. He was thirty years old and badly wounded when he jumped out of the *Polecat* at about 1400 hours over total cloud cover, expecting to land in the freezing North Sea. S/Sgt. Darter was shot through his right arm and leg and experienced serious loss of blood while collapsed on the extremely cold floor of the radio room since 1325 hours (nearly twenty-five minutes before Doral found him).

Sgt. Eugene Darter was the "grandpa" on the crew, as the other crew members were several years younger. He owned a security business and was an undercover government investigator in the Los Angeles area prior to the war and obviously knew how to survive if at all possible, but he was seriously wounded and had left a lot of blood on the freezing floor of the radio room. (Photo credit United States Army Air Corps)

1310 to 1325 Hours: Hit during Fighter Attack

S/Sgt. Darter was hit during the fighter attack several minutes after "bombs away" over the submarine facilities' target in Bremen as he was shooting his 50-caliber machine gun out the top of the radio room hatch at an attacking enemy aircraft coming in from the tail. Most likely, Darter was hit in the right arm by a 20-mm shell from an attacking ME109 that also hit and shattered the radio room. Eugene collapsed onto the floor of the radio room and remained there for nearly twenty-five minutes, experiencing the loss of blood without an oxygen mask. Fortunately, the *Polecat* continued to lose altitude to below ten thousand feet quickly, or he would surely have died from lack of oxygen. Doral said there was blood all over the shattered radio room when he found him. This occurred during the enemy aircraft attack about fifteen minutes after bombs away, so this attack occurred just before 1325 when the American escort of P-47s and P-51s showed up and drove off the enemy fighters. Waist gunner Charlie Schreiner confirmed that he saw Darter get hit in the radio room as he was standing on an ammunition box, shooting his machine gun out the top of the aircraft at an enemy aircraft. He fell to the freezing floor and then lay on his back in severe pain and shock, holding his arm and leg. Perhaps the subfreezing temperatures prevented him from bleeding to death during this time period.

Approximately 1400 Hours: Bailout into the Unknown

Eugene Darter had collapsed on the floor of the *Polecat* for nearly twenty-five minutes (until approximately 1352 hours) when Doral found him and administered first aid (stopped his bleeding arm with a tourniquet and gave him a shot of morphine on his wound) and helped him get on his feet and ready to bail out.

Hupp immediately realized a serious problem. Darter's right arm was useless, and he could not pull his chest pack parachute metal pin with that hand. It was very difficult, if not, impossible, to pull it with his left hand, and thus, bailing out would be fatal. To help visualize the situation, observe the photo of a statue of an airman at the Cambridge American Military Cemetery. Note the following:

- The parachute harness with straps that go over his shoulders and down his sides and are attached to other straps that go between his legs. Note also the horizontal chest strap (with the buckle in the center) that holds the vertical straps together.
- Just below the horizontal chest strap, there are two semicircular eyelets where the two hard steel snaps on the chest pack parachute are attached.
- The airman is carrying a chest pack parachute in his left hand. This chute is snapped onto the two semicircular eyelets on the harness just below the horizontal chest strap so that the airman can pull the pin with his right hand. Note the metal pin on the parachute that must be pulled with the right hand to activate the chute after leaving the aircraft.
- Underneath the parachute harness is the (noninflated) Mae West life jacket. Note the two vertical chords with small balls on their ends near his waist that the airman must pull to activate each half of the life vest.

Hupp quickly came up with the brilliant idea of snapping on his chest parachute upside down so he could pull the metal pin with his left hand. He mentioned this to pilot Fred Delbern in their brief discussion after Delbern came out of the cockpit to check on the men and the plane. Hupp stated that after he got Darter up and ready, he was "quite lively." He reported that as he and the others were getting ready to bail out, Darter moved with great difficulty from the radio room back, squeezing past the ball turret, past the waist gunners Schreiner and Lee and tail gunner McKeegan (who had come up from his position), to the back right door of the aircraft. As he passed the waist windows, he noticed thick smoke coming from the #2 engine, which greatly alarmed him about the aircraft blowing up. Darter decided to get out of the plane as quickly as possible and looked back at Hupp and said, "Doral, you remember what we talked about?" Doral told me he was referring to their discussions about the high risk of the air war, and if this war continued, they could all be hurt or worse. Hupp said, "Yes." Darter, although white and weak from loss of blood, managed a smile and said, "I'll be all right."

An Army Air Force airman statue located along the Wall of the Missing at
the Cambridge American Military Cemetery in England (note his parachute
harness, life vest, and chest pack parachute in his right hand, which snaps onto
the two snaps on his harness just below the horizontal cross harness strap)
(Photo credit M. I. Darter)

Then he waddled over to the open rear right door (where the rest
of the men in the back of the aircraft would soon bail out) and without
hesitation jumped out of the stricken aircraft into the white unknown
below. Doral was surprised because he had told Eugene to wait until
he was ready and they would go out together. Doral and the others
immediately looked out the waist windows and door and watched as
he quickly pulled the pin with his left hand, and it worked, his chute
opened, and he dropped down into the thick cloud cover just below,
vanishing from their sight.[2] They would never see Eugene Darter again.

The frightening condition of the *Polecat* may have caused Darter to
get out before it exploded as so many B-17s had done (several on this

mission). However, not waiting for the rest of the crew to bail out and landing in the cold ocean alone could also be disastrous. Charlie told me that the reason Darter left the aircraft quickly might have been that he was bleeding so badly and was so weak (Charlie said that Darter was weak and his face was white from loss of blood) that he would have become unconscious and died if he didn't get some medical attention fast. If he jumped, he had a chance of getting medical attention from the Germans or the Dutch. This is similar to the comment made by crewmate Ed Woollen that if he had not jumped out quickly, he would have bled to death on the aircraft. I have met several airmen who experienced this same situation and bailed out to try to get timely medical help, and they received it in Dutch or German hospitals and saved their lives.

Doral Hupp (and Charlie Schreiner) observed the following surprising event at that point:

> *Just after Eugene jumped out, I got my parachute and was putting it on with the Mae West and I looked out the window on the left side and saw a P-47 pulled up beside us approximately 100 yards out. I waved at him and he tipped his wings and flew away.*[2]

This apparently was their US escort who had driven off the German fighters and protected them for the last thirty minutes all the way to the Dutch coast. The pilot of the P-47 saw Darter bail out and may have recorded the coordinates of the *Polecat* when he saw it on fire and losing altitude. It may be possible to identify its squadron (either the 4th, 355th, or 356th fighter group provided protection on this mission) and locate the base interrogation reports.

Tail gunner Bob McKeegan stated the following after the war in 1945:

> *Darter bailed out "somewhere between Bremen and the Isle of Texel. I assisted him into his parachute and to bail out." He stated that Darter was injured in his "right leg, side and arm hit badly with shrapnel." He stated, "His chute was seen to open. In all probability landed in the North Sea. We were above the clouds and couldn't see the ground. I followed him out a few minutes later and landed on the isle of Texel of the Friesian Island chain."*[3]

During crew interrogation at Horham base that night, a very interesting observation was made by the Hubb crew of the 95th BG B Group (the same bombing group as the *Polecat* that day):

> One chute out of B-17 just after we reached coast of Holland. This B-17 had feathered prop before target and went on over it and was last seen ½ hour before we reached English coast.[4]

This B-17 is clearly the *Lonesome Polecat II* (the feathered prop before Bremen was a distinct sight and was observed by several crews and reported during interrogation back at the base). That one chute out after the coast of Holland is believed to be that of S/Sgt. Eugene F. Darter. The Hubb crew reached Texel coastline at 1359, so they saw Darter's parachute "just after" at about, say, 1400. Where was the *Lonesome Polecat* at that time? The aircraft crossed the Dutch coast/Wadden Sea at about 1353 and would have been approaching the Texel coast at 1400. All this indicates that my brother bailed out and came down somewhere in the Wadden Sea not far from the Texel coastline.

Sighting of Lonesome Polecat II over Oost (east side of Texel)

A piece of information regarding the flight path of the Polecat was obtained when I interviewed Mr. Jack Betsema in 2002, a resident of Texel (brother to Gerrit Van Betsema), and he told how his father (Gerrit Betsema) had told him about a B-17 that came low over his village of Oost on the east (Wadden Sea) side of the island, with one engine stopping and one smoking. If this was the *Polecat* (it was a very foggy day, but there could have been a break in the clouds), then it would help to establish the flight line of the aircraft between Oost on the eastern coast and De Koog on the western (North Sea) coast. This is certainly a reasonable course due west from Bremen and a likely location for the *Polecat* to cross over the eastern edge of Texel.

1400 Hours: Landing in the freezing Wadden Sea

When he left the aircraft, Darter had on boxer shorts and a T-shirt, long johns, then regular-issue pants and shirt, a two-piece electrically heated flying suit, and finally gabardine flying suite and an A-2 leather jacket. He also had prepared a medicine bag according to Hupp. He also had his non-inflated Mae West life jacket under his parachute harness when he bailed out, as all of the men expected to land in the ocean (see the airman statue for typical clothing worn by the crew). Hupp had snapped on his chest pack parachute upside down so he could pull the pin with his left arm. Doral estimates that the *Polecat* was at four-thousand- to five-thousand-foot elevation. The remaining crew watched from the aircraft and observed that his chute opened and he entered the thick undercast below and disappeared.

If his splash down in the Wadden Sea went according to training (note that the crew never practiced bailing out and had only limited training in procedures for landing in water), he would have done the following according to the *Pilots' Information File 1944* had he been physically able:

1. Pull yourself well back in the sling and undo the leg straps.
2. As soon as you are in the water, release one side of the chest pack (parachute) from the harness. (Note that to release the chest chute one must depress the two stiff steel spring-loaded clips on each side of the chute. This requires considerable strength and two hands.)
3. Then unfasten the chest strap (unfasten the snap on the horizontal harness which would allow the life vest to fully inflate).
4. Inflate the Mae West, one half at a time, but never until the chest strap is unfastened. Either half will support you.
   Get away from the parachute and shroud lines and stay away!

Given his major loss of blood after being hit, the below freezing air temperatures in the aircraft, the near-freezing Wadden Sea temperature, and the trauma of the injuries and coming down in the freezing temperature from the aircraft, how likely is it that Eugene Darter could have accomplished all of the above?

It is possible that after he entered the water in his weakened state, his parachute came down on him, and he was unable to get out from under it and unsnap it from his harness with only one arm. He would have drowned quickly under the chute if this happened. However, with a strong wind blowing, the parachute should not have landed on him but out in the direction the wind was blowing (e.g., out to sea).

The steel spring-loaded snaps connecting the parachute to the harness surrounding his body are very stiff and it is doubtful if he could have unsnapped them in the cold water with his right arm shot and useless and his left hand weakened from loss of a lot of blood and near freezing temperature. Not unsnapping the parachute meant that we was strongly connected to the parachute. Next he should have unfastened the snap on the horizontal harness that would allow the life vest to fully inflate. As noted above, you must unfasten the horizontal harness snap prior to inflating the vest or your chest would be practically crushed.

The Wadden Sea water was cold (air temperature on December 16, 1943, was just above freezing, 32 °F or 0 °C); and with wind, there would have been significant waves. He would then have had to swim toward the shore tethered to the parachute (if he could see through the fog), but with only one functioning arm and fully clothed, it would have been almost impossible to swim long. Eugene had only a few minutes to maintain consciousness to survive in the cold water even if he got himself detached from the parachute and inflated his life jacket.

The Wadden Sea

The area of the Wadden Sea along the flight path is very shallow near Texel Island. Eons ago, this area was a marsh. Depending on the tide (which changes twice per day), it might range from a high of three to six feet (one to two meters) of seawater to a low of almost no water in areas as shown on topographic maps on the flight path. Thus, it is possible that if Darter splashed down during low tide, he would have walked on the bottom of the Wadden Sea into the shore. If he landed at high tide, he would have begun swimming into the shore but, within minutes, would have suffered from hypothermia, shock from his wounds, and weakness from blood loss, and he could not have made it far from where he landed before blacking out.

During my first visit to Texel in September 2000 with Johan Graas, it was a very foggy day with low visibility (fishing boats could be seen only within less than a mile out in the Wadden Sea). It was unlikely that anyone could possibly have seen a man parachuting into the Wadden Sea if more than a short distance from shore. And even if someone did, there are no rescue boats within thirty minutes of this location. Thus, a landing in the Wadden Sea in this area was a hopeless situation for Eugene Darter. My finding of any more information about his last moments was hopeless indeed.

The following aerial photo shows the potential flight path of the B-17F across the Wadden Sea and Texel Island. Note the shallow water of the Wadden Sea along the flight path where the sandy bottom can be seen at low tide. At low tide, the water depth would be very shallow; but at high tide, water depth would be approximately 1.5 meters (five feet, ten inches). High or low tide would have made a life or death difference for my brother.

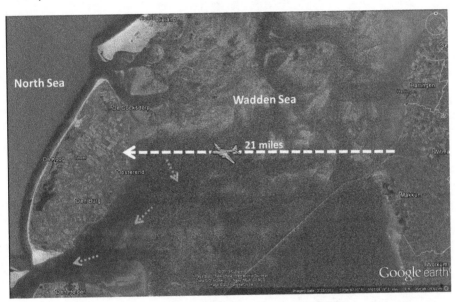

Aerial photo of Texel Island surrounded by the North Sea on the left and Wadden Sea on the right, showing the bottom of the Wadden Sea during low tide. The dashed line shows the *Polecat*'s approximate flight path. The arrows show possible splashdown locations and the path of Eugene Darter's remains following the flow of water. (Image credit Google Earth)

Tide Records for Wadden Sea

Amazingly, the Dutch Waterworks Bureau located the tide elevation record on the Wadden Sea for December 16, 1943, as shown below. The horizontal axis is the time on a twenty-four-hour clock. The vertical scale is the surface elevation of the surface of the Wadden Sea at three locations. The record shows that indeed and unfortunately, the water level of the Wadden Sea was just receding from its high tide at the time of the splashdown of S/Sgt. Eugene F. Darter at 1400 hours (or 2:00 p.m.). Thus, he landed just as the water current was going outward as shown on the graph with the lowering of the water surface. Water depth between low- and high-tide change was 1.4 meters (fifty-five inches), which is just less than Eugene's height of sixty-five inches.

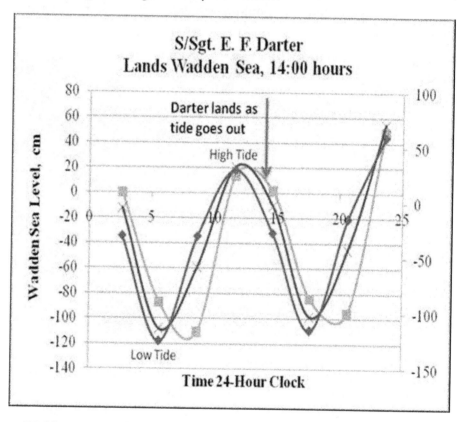

Wadden Sea tide records at three locations near Texel Island, December 16, 1943 (Data credit Netherlands Waterworks Bureau)

With the high tide receding at that time, his remains would have been carried out further into the deeper channels of the Wadden Sea. These deeper channels can be seen in the photo of this area at low tide. His body may have become lodged in one of these deeper channels and eventually become covered over with sand and never surfaced again if he did not inflate his Mae West. On the other hand, if he did pull his Mae West chord and inflate his life jacket it would have floated his body likely tethered to his parachute and his remains would have floated for days or longer in the sea.

Since the Germans prohibited fishing in this area, the remains would not likely have been picked up by a fishing boat and buried near a Wadden Sea port. Another possibility is that they were carried out into the Wadden Sea channel and then from there out into the North Sea through either the north or south channel.

Experience of Harold Kious

The actual experience of an airman who bailed out over the Wadden Sea in wintertime would obviously provide the most likely answer as to what S/Sgt. Eugene Darter experienced. I met Lt. Harold Kious on Texel one summer. He bailed out of his B-17 and landed in the Wadden Sea only about one-fourth mile off the coast of Texel (just a few miles south of where Eugene came down) on a cold March 4, 1943, and would have drowned if not rescued by some brave Dutchmen on a ferryboat. Here is his account of his experience:

> When the pilot told me to abandon the aircraft, I started towards the rear of the airplane. I was wearing a seat pack parachute and could not "squeeze" through the small bomb-bay catwalk. I then decided to step around the catwalk. Just as I stepped to the edge of the bomb-bay door centrifugal force pushed me to the floor of the bomb bay. The aircraft had probably gone into a spin. I did not have the strength to pull myself up. The bomb bay doors had large jagged holes in them where our bombs had fallen from the shackles during some violent evasive action we had taken earlier in the flight. I could not pull myself up from the bottom of the floor and chose to drop through the hole in the bomb bay.
>
> I drifted slowly along the underside of the airplane. I approached the ball-turret and pushed off from it into the air. I counted to 10 about 2 and 1/2 times and opened the parachute. I was still very high in the air and could see the Island of Texel. It looked about the size of a postage stamp. There was an easterly wind of about 15 to 20 miles per hour blowing.

As I neared the water I unbuckled one of my leg straps. As soon as I touched the water I unbuckled the other leg strap and then unbuckled the chest strap (of the parachute harness). I landed in the water about 1/4 mile from shore. I could see a few people walking along the dike.

I was a fairly good swimmer and felt I could swim to shore. I inflated my Mae West (life vest) and began to swim. After a few strokes my vision began to blacken. I rolled onto my back to rest. I again tried to swim and the same blackness began to occur. I realized that I was about to become unconscious and rolled onto by back each time that blackness occurred. This happened about four times. On the last time that I was on by back, I became unconscious.

I awakened about three to four hours later in the German headquarters on Texel Island. During my time in the water I felt no discomfort. I do not recall that the water was cold although it was reported to me later that the water temperature was 38 degrees F. I later learned that I had been fished from the water by three Dutchmen who were onboard the ferry boat "Dokter Wagemaker." Had it not been for their courage and determination I would have drowned the same as two others of my crewmembers (who also landed out further in the Wadden Sea just ahead of him).[26]

Note that these Dutchmen took their lives in their own hands to do this against the orders of a German officer on board the ferry. Kious returned to Texel regularly to meet and express gratitude to his rescuers for many years, becoming quite famous on Texel until his recent death in 2008 at over ninety years of age. Parts of his aircraft have been located in the Wadden Sea and are now on display in various museums on Texel and North Holland.

Harold told me several times that I met him on Texel that my brother would not have suffered pain in the water as he would just have blacked out and never recovered. This knowledge brought our family some relief.

Bit by bit and piece by piece, we have begun to put the puzzle together about what happened to my brother Eugene as we continue our search on Texel Island and out into the Wadden Sea.

CHAPTER 13

A MIRACLE OCCURS AS FOUR CREW COME THROUGH UNDERCAST

Texel Island is a beautiful, peaceful place today, but in 1943, it was heavily occupied by the Nazis. As part of the northernmost portion of the Atlantic Wall defense against the Allies, the island lies about twenty-five miles out along the flight path from the main Dutch coast across the Wadden Sea. The island is roughly twenty miles long and six miles wide.

A plaque at the Texel cemetery reads,

> *During WW II, 23 allied bombers were shot down over or close to Texel. The crews found their last resting place in this cemetery in Den Burg, with the exception of the American dead who were transferred to Margraten Cemetery (south Netherlands) after the war. Survivors were sometimes saved by the local people or were cared for by them in the first instance. In some cases, this has led to enduring friendships.*

Records show that many bodies of drowned US Army Air Force and Royal Air Force flight crews were washed ashore on Texel and other islands surrounded by the North Sea and the Wadden Sea.

Texel was directly on the return flight path for the 95th BG. The main 95th BG formation bomber stream experienced some flak as they passed over the cloud- and fog-covered island at 1358 (A formation) to 1359 (B formation) hours on December 16, 1943.

Several minutes later, the severely damaged, straggling *Polecat* approached the island at a much lower elevation of five thousand feet. Pilot Fred Delbern, with fatally injured Don Neff slumped over in the copilot's seat and five crew members in the rear of the B-17F were frantically preparing to bail out before the smoking and vibrating aircraft blew up from fire in the #2 engine. The crew members could see nothing except solid cloud cover below them, and none knew where they were but suspected they were by now over the North Sea since they had been flying for some time after leaving Bremen approximately forty minutes prior.

Bail Out into the Unknown

Charlie Schreiner related the sequence of bailout from the rear of the plane:

> *Of the crewmembers from the aft of the ship Darter was the first to leave and his parachute blossomed perfectly. McKeegan, Hupp, and Lee followed in respective order a few minutes later after we had checked parachute harnesses and dingies. I followed in short order and waved to Lee after my chute had opened.*

The altitude at bailout was estimated by Doral at four to five thousand feet. Thick undercast fog and cloud cover existed below, so it did not take long for the crew members to reach the ground. As the four crew members (after Darter) each passed through the thick clouds and fog, they were astounded to suddenly see the ground just below them. Each of the men had expected to splash down and likely die in the ocean as so many flight crews had preceded them in the frigid waters of the North Sea. December 16, 1943, was a very cold, cloudy, and foggy day on Texel Island, with temperatures hovering around freezing.

Bob McKeegan landed near the southern end of the Texel airport near Muyweg Road. Doral Hupp and Frank Lee landed further west toward the North Sea in the flat cultivated area (Zuid Eierland) prior to the large hilly dune area just before the North Sea. This dune area consists of thick grass and shrub-covered high dunes (hills) along the North Sea beach that is about one mile (1.6 km) wide.

Charlie Schreiner (the last person left in the back of the aircraft) hesitated a few more seconds before bailing out and landed farther west in the high dune area, less than a half a mile from the North Sea. He hit the ground pretty hard and was knocked out for a few seconds.

As Doral passed through the clouds he spotted the ground only about five hundred feet below. Frank landed on a large mound and Doral Hupp on a smaller one. They both hit hard only a few hundred yards from each other, but quickly got up and found a nearby hole beneath some bushes, crawled into the hole, buried their parachutes in the hole, and hid until it was dark. They could see German soldiers searching for them as they peered out of the hole. Although Doral landed about one to two miles (1.6 to 3.2 km) from the North Sea due to the hilly topography and fog, he did not see the ocean and did not know that they were even on an island. After it was dark, they got out of the hole and found a nearby farmhouse with a turnip patch, so they promptly dug up some turnips and ate them. Hupp remembers the farmhouse had a dark roof, trees, and a fence.

What the men did not know is that they had also unfortunately landed near some German barracks, so there were soldiers nearby who heard the stricken B-17F fly low overhead and were searching for crew who bailed out. Bob McKeegan was captured immediately upon landing by German soldiers and then taken quite a distance to the location where Charlie Schreiner landed in the hilly dunes and pastures near the North Sea.

Hupp and Lee avoided immediate capture by hiding in the hole for several hours, but when they emerged from the hole after dark, they were captured together by the Hitler Youth group in the woods by a farmhouse. They were taken to a small building just north of the farmhouse, where Charlie and Bob had been taken. The next day, all four Americans were taken off Texel Island and transferred by train to Amsterdam.

Charlie was the last one to bail out of the *Polecat*. The parachute ride down was very quiet. When Charlie broke through the clouds and fog, he was amazed to see land just below. He had on his Mae West life jacket as he believed they were over the North Sea. Charlie came down on land and hit so hard that it knocked him out for a few minutes. He gave himself a shot of morphine in his wrist and knee for pain as both had been hit by flak during the Bremen bomb run. As can be seen on the map, he did land fairly close to the western edge of Texel Island. Had he hesitated a few additional seconds, he would have been over the cold North Sea and would likely have died from hypothermia.

He was wounded in the knee and hand and was in a lot of pain. Cloud ceiling was low, and there was fog. Within two to three minutes, German soldiers were on him, and he surrendered and gave up his gun and became a POW. He soon saw Bob McKeegan, who was also captured by the German soldiers and brought over in the dune area to where Charlie landed.

The two Americans were then taken by the German soldiers back through an entranceway to the dunes. Charlie remembers that they were met by a Dutch farmer to whom he gave his parachute in the presence of the German soldiers because it was difficult to carry with his injured hand and leg. He noticed that the farmer was wearing wooden shoes. Amazingly, Johan Grass was able to locate the farmer, Mr. P. K. Stark (who, in 2001, when we met, just turned eighty-three years old and lives in Den Burg, Texel), who on that day was out on the sand dunes working on his farm. On June 22, 2001, Mr. Stark met with Johan Graas and me and traveled to the location where he saw the two crew members.

Here is P. K. Stark's story of the events of that day:

> On that day [December 16, 1943] in the afternoon I was working on my land in the dunes. It was very foggy and it was difficult to see things far away. One moment I saw something colored white in the fog. I thought it was German soldiers taking a sheep of mine with them, but it was one or two parachutes carried by the crewmembers. I was walking very fast, back over the dunes to the small farmer's path and walking to the north. Here was the entrance for coming into the dunes. One minute later the German soldiers were coming out of the dunes with two prisoners. One was wounded and was walking badly [note that Charlie Schreiner was wounded in his kneecap and hand and was in a lot of pain]. One of the German soldiers took his parachute, but the German officer told him not to do that. On that moment I said to the German officer that I would like to have the parachute, as it was too heavy for the wounded man. On the wounded man's jacket, on the front side, I read Schre . . . or something like that, I can't remember the entire word.

Mr. P. K. Stark (Left) and Michael Darter on top of the high dunes on Texel on June 23, 2001, looking toward the west and the North Sea where Charles Schreiner landed (upper right portion of photo). Mr. Stark carried Charlie's parachute as he was too injured to carry it. (Photo credit M. I. Darter)

We then were walking for 1 mile to the north to the German barracks. One of the Germans asked me if I had seen one or more airplanes. I told him that I never saw an airplane. After this I was going home and heard later that on another place some other crewmembers got prisoner by the Germans. After that I went back to my farmhouse.[28]

Mr. P. K. Stark had met S/Sgt. Charles Schreiner and S/Sgt. Robert McKeegan carrying their parachutes and surrounded by German soldiers coming out of these dunes through an opening half a mile to the far right in the photos (bike and walking trails exist there today). The road that is located at the entrance to the dunes where Mr. Stark met the two crew members and German soldiers is named Muyweg Road and runs along the southern end of the Texel International Airport. Both Doral and Frank were captured near a home along Muyweg Road. I asked Mr. Stark if he remembers wearing wooden shoes, and he stated that it was common to wear wooden shoes at that time and that he probably had them on. The North Sea is about one mile from this location between beach marker #23 and #24.

Temporary Prisoners on Texel

All four crew members that landed on Texel Island on that cold December 16, 1943, at about 1400 hours (2:00 p.m.) were captured within a time span of a few minutes to five hours and were taken to a German army facility and held overnight. They did not know at that time how they had miraculously landed on a small island in the North Sea and thereby saved their lives. They could not see land below as everything was totally obscured by clouds. Later, they all realized how truly miraculous their lives were saved by coming down on the island. They avoided certain death in the freezing Wadden Sea or the North Sea.

The four crewmen were incredibly grateful they had survived thus far, but saddened that Eugene, Fred, and Don were not with them that night. Of course, they did not tell the Germans about their other crewmates. They knew that Pete, Loren, and Eddie had bailed out over mainland Europe. They also knew that Eugene had bailed out just before they did and that pilots Fred and Don were still flying the *Polecat* toward England when they were last seen.

The next day, they were all taken off the island and transferred to Amsterdam by train to begin another phase of their life as prisoners of war (POWs) with a very uncertain and unknown future. They would spend many hours as POWs wondering and discussing what happened and praying for their crewmates on that fateful day.

General Flight Path of the Polecat

A map of Texel Island is shown below with the approximate flight path of the *Polecat* as it crossed the island from east to west between the villages of Oost on the east and De Koog on the west. We had now discovered (with the invaluable help of Johan Grass and Doral and Charlie who were still alive at that time) the General locations where the crewmen landed (from right to left): my brother Eugene somewhere out in the Wadden Sea; next, Bob McKeegan, Doral Hupp, and Frank Lee safely in the middle of the island; and finally, Charlie Schreiner just before the North

Sea. The end of the journey for pilots Delbern and Neff and the B-17F came sometime after all crew had bailed out, and they headed out over the North Sea at 1403 hours on December 16, 1943, about one-half mile north of De Koog village.

We had truly uncovered a lot of the remarkable story since the fall of 2000 when Johan Grass and I had first visited Texel and, after walking the beach and dunes, were overwhelmed at the odds of ever finding out anything about the final minutes of the flight of the *Polecat* and her brave crew. By now, I had come to "know" most of the crew besides my brother quite well from all the interviews with the four survivors and the families of the others, along with all the National Archives information available. But there was still so much more that we wanted to learn about each of their fateful lives. Our journey continues with renewed energy. I was gaining hope against hope that I would learn more about my brother's final moments.

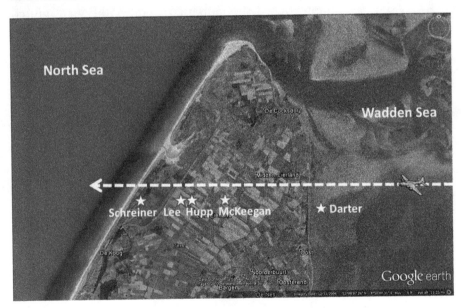

Map of Texel Island showing the general flight path of the *Polecat* and the approximate locations where the crew landed (Image credit Google Earth)

CHAPTER 14

DECISION TIME: BAIL NOW, FLY ENGLAND, OR DITCH NORTH SEA?

As the *Polecat* approached the Dutch coast at 1350 hours, injured pilot Fred Delbern was grateful to have made it this far, having fought off numerous German fighter attacks and antiaircraft flak hits and lost nearly twenty thousand feet of altitude. However, he had grave concern that the badly damaged *Polecat* could return all the way to the English coast, which was over a hundred miles and at least forty-five minutes flying time away. The most dangerous situation was the #2 engine fire trailing thick black smoke that posed a grave threat as it could trigger an explosion that would destroy the aircraft and kill anyone still on board. Crewmate Charlie Schreiner said that "the engine fires were melting the metal off the wings and the plane was vibrating violently from the windmilling prop on #3 engine."[36] If Charlie was correct in describing the #2 as also "windmilling," this would have made the situation even more untenable and could have resulted in the prop fracturing from the engine and severely damaging the aircraft. Charlie also said that fuel was running very low and the aircraft could not have made it back to England.

Fred was also very much distressed at the fatal injury of his friend and able copilot Don Neff slumped next to him in the cockpit, and of course Delbern was also hit in his arm by flak, and his face was blackened. He barely had the strength to control the damaged aircraft. Fred had gotten through on the intercom to Doral in the ball turret a few minutes earlier and ordered him to check out the back of the aircraft, but he had not heard from him and urgently needed to know the damage situation. So he switched on the autopilot and got out of the cockpit holding his injured arm and opened the door to the bomb bay and looked back through into the shattered radio room. He immediately saw Doral aiding badly wounded Eugene Darter and helping him put on his parachute. He talked briefly to Hupp through the length of the open bomb bay doors as Hupp related,

> *While bandaging Eugene, the pilot, Fred Delbern appeared outside the cockpit and I spoke very briefly with him regarding the co-pilot and Eugene. He said something like, "forget about the co-pilot" [this indicated to Doral that Don was fatally injured]. The pilot went back up front after a few moments talking to me. His face black tinted as if there had been a fire up front. That was the only time that he appeared to the rear of the plane. He closed the door between the bomb bay and the pilot section of the plane.[2]*

Charlie Schreiner gives a more detailed account in his November 1945 letter to Delbern's wife:

> *Delbern had been hit in the left arm and he eventually crawled back through the cat-walk to the radio room to see how we were making out. Our inter-phone system had been knocked out of commission way back at the target so I guess he didn't know exactly what was going on in the rear.*
>
> *Delbern sized up the situation and orally gave Doral the order that "the ship was to be abandoned immediately." The engine fires were melting the metal off the wings and the plane was vibrating violently from the windmilling prop on #3 engine. Even if the plane had not disintegrated apart in the air from the vibrations, our fuel had run so low that we couldn't get halfway over the channel with two engines.[36]*

Given what Delbern saw and heard, he again made the same decision as he had over Germany when they were hit and under severe attack to get the remaining crew out of the aircraft as soon as possible, as they could not make it back. Charlie describes what happened next after Eugene, Bob, Doral, and Frank bailed out:

I followed in short order and waved to Lee after my chute had opened. I turned my eyes skyward, the plane was still flying toward England and leaving a trail of smoke as it flew. In my thoughts as I glided slowly downward toward the foggy cloud formations that hung 450 to 500 feet from the ground was a great question. What did they intend to do? They had not left the plane, what decision had Del and Neff made?

They had three alternatives: (1) they could leave the ship by chute, (2) they could continue straight toward England and ditch the plane in the North Sea and hope for English Air-Sea Rescue, (3) they could swing the ship around and attempt to crash-land on the enemy coast.[36]

This was the last time anyone saw Fred or Don, and the question remains: what did they do?

Crew Statements

First of all, the following are statements made by various crew members after their release from the POW camp in 1945 (MACR 1558)[3] and more recently in personal interviews (2000-07) regarding the condition of the pilots and what may of happened.

> **Bob McKeegan statement (MACR 1558 in 1945):** *Ball turret gunner (Hupp) reported him (Delbern) wounded in right arm. He was last seen going forward from radio room. Sgt. Hupp reported he saw Delbern come into radio room as he was assisting Sgt. Darter who was wounded . . . He went forward to the flight deck. No one saw him after that. The pilot always claimed he would never bail out. I believe he stayed at the controls even after all had bailed out.*

> **Royal (Pete) Jackson Statements (MACR 1558):** *Lt. Delbern told me in training that he would never attempt a jump but would risk staying with plane for forced landing. A German interrogator claims plane crashed into sea off enemy coast. Would give no information regarding bodies.*

Charles J. Schreiner Statements (MACR 1558): Besides the above statement in his November 1945 letter, Charlie wrote the following in his MACR statement: *I believe he (Delbern) tried to ditch the plane. The last time I saw it, it was mushing down toward the sea.* [Note that Charlie was the last person to bail out and thus the last person to see the aircraft.] *Germans said they found the ship and found 2 bodies in it. They wanted to know their names so they could notify the United States.*

Junius E. Woollen statements (MACR 1558): *The last time Woollen saw the pilot and copilot they were both in their places. Both pilot and copilot as well as radioman had been wounded by enemy action. Pilot Delbern had been hit by gunfire, fatally I believe.*

Was he [Delbern] injured? *Yes, hit in arm, leg, and abdomen.* Where was he when last seen? *In his seat trying to control plane.*

Any hearsay information: *He felt that he could possibly get the plane back always, and had often said he would not bail out, but would try to fly the plane down, even though he ordered the rest of the crew to bail out. He told me this often during our training.*

Based wholly on supposition and what I saw before I bailed out, I think the pilot stayed with the plane too long and that it exploded, or at least became uncontrollable and made it impossible to get out.

Loren Dodson: Loren Dodson told me that just before he bailed out of the aircraft near Leer, Germany, neither of the pilots were injured that he could see and he was directly behind the cockpit and spoke with the pilot.[2] Loren Dodson was interrogated by a German officer in Frankfurt who told him that his plane crashed into the North Sea. Thus, there must have been a German record that documented this incident.

Shattered Lonesome Polecat II

Secondly, the *Polecat* was in a disastrous situation, just as it was four weeks prior returning from a similar mission to Bremen, Germany.

It is truly amazing that the aircraft did not explode in the air (as many did) long before reaching Texel Island with this extent of damage. The condition of the *Polecat* is summarized below as described by the crew prior to the bailout. Fred knew he could not fly the *Polecat* for another thirty to forty-five minutes required to make the English coast.

1400 Hours: Approaching the North Sea

High above in the sky, unknown to Fred, Hptm. Alfred Grislawski, a highly decorated German ace pilot with 132 shoot downs, was also carefully watching the smoking B-17F cross-cloud-covered Texel Island. He noted that the American P-47 escort flew off and the bailouts and waited for his chance to dive down and make another kill out in the North Sea if the aircraft continued on toward England.

Note on engine numbering: The engines are numbered (assume that you are sitting on the tail of the aircraft, looking forward to the front of the aircraft). Starting at the far left side is #1 (outboard), #2 (inboard), #3 (inboard), and #4 (outboard).

1. No. 1 engine running
2. No. 2 engine hit by enemy aircraft, trailing thick black smoke, fire melting metal off wings
3. No. 3 engine feathered, shot out by flak just before reaching target, but reportedly windmilling
4. No. 4 engine running
5. Windshield on copilot's side shattered from enemy aircraft fire
6. Large hole in wing between nos. 3 and 4 engines. This hole would have reduced the lift on this side of the aircraft, contributing to the loss of altitude.
7. The floor of the plane was littered with many spent brass .50-caliber casings.
8. Wings and fuselage riddled with jagged holes of varying sizes from flak and enemy aircraft
9. The tail portion of the plane was destroyed including tail gunner's position.
10. The top turret was hit and shattered, as well as the radio room destroyed by enemy aircraft fire. The nose of the aircraft has also been hit by flak and by fighters.

11. The bomb bay doors were still open, and the plane was vibrating violently.
12. Fuel had run so low that the B-17 couldn't get halfway over the channel with two engines.

Lonesome Polecat II (B-17F) Over Texel Island

Painting of the stricken *Lonesome Polecat II* as it passed over Texel Island on December 16, 1943, moments before crashing into the North Sea based on crew information (Image credit artist John Blott, Horham, UK)

Pilot Fred Delbern was very averse to parachuting out of the aircraft. He had told several crew members that if they were hit during combat and had to abandon ship. He would not bail out but would always bring it down to ditch either on land or in the sea. Fred had attended the briefing that morning where the planned return flight path from Bremen was directly west and over a Dutch island called Texel, where the formation was to turn southwest toward England and their home bases.

Fred had been searching the cloud cover below for a break to establish his location. Looking up through his windshield, Fred could still see the silver specks of the American bomber stream far above. Looking down, there was cloud cover as far as he could see. Then suddenly, he looked down, and a hole in the cloud cover appeared, and he spotted what looked like a white beach below. Could this the Texel beach that runs more than twenty miles along the North Sea edge? He immediately made the decision that he told his crew many times he would do in such a situation: ditch the wounded *Polecat* in the sea near the beach. This might also allow him to get his wounded copilot to a hospital if he was still alive as well as himself as his arm was hit by flak.

1400 Hours: Turning Around and Bringing the Polecat Down

The German ace hovering far above the *Polecat* never got the chance to swoop down because Lt. Delbern immediately began a sharp banking turn to the left (or southward) in a downward spiral, bringing the *Polecat* quickly down through the cloud cover close to the ground.

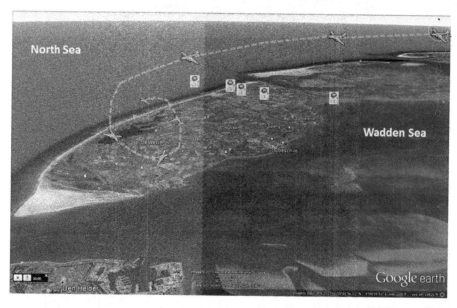

Path of the *Lonesome Polecat II* B-17F as the five remaining crew bailed out and four of them miraculously came down over the island. Pilot Fred Delbern spotted the North Sea Texel beach through the clouds and banked to the left in a downward spiral, attempting to ditch just off the Texel North Sea beach. (Image credit Google Earth)

Piece of Burning Aircraft Falls on Farm

Hans Eelman, longtime resident of Texel, knew a farmer named Wilem Dalmeiger, who lived just southeast from De Koog. Dalmeiger told Hans a few years ago before he died that on the afternoon of December 16, 1943, he heard the roar of a big aircraft just over his farm but could not see it due to the thick sea fog. Then he found melted pieces of aluminum that had fallen from the aircraft onto his land (from the #2 engine). The location of Dalmeiger's farm southeast of De Koog village fits the downward spiral flight path as the *Polecat* made a left-hand loop as shown.

As the *Polecat* completed the downward spiral and leveled out just above the rooftops and head back west to the North Sea beach to ditch, Fred observed a small village (De Koog) directly ahead through his wind screen. He managed to keep the B-17F just over the tops of the roofs of the village where he saw German soldiers shooting at him. But suddenly, directly ahead of the aircraft was a high dune hill just before the sea, and Fred desperately pulled back on the stick with his one good arm as hard as he could. The *Polecat* shuttered mightily but lifted up and just barely skimmed the top of the dune. Recently, a new home has been built at this exact location on the dune, which would have been directly hit by the B-17 had it been there in 1943 as observed by an eyewitness Michele Binsbergen standing in the village. Fred was immediately faced with another row of high dunes, which he easily cleared, and finally there was the North Sea with a wide pristine white beach that he had spotted through the clouds.

The Final Moments

Fred, now very weak and exhausted from loss of blood and the huge strain of flying the damaged B-17 all the way from Bremen, sharply banked the burning, smoking, and vibrating *Polecat* to the left again, trying to level out but wildly gyrating from side to side parallel to the North Sea Texel beach, losing altitude rapidly.

A high wind speed of 15 to 25 mph pushed the large waves crashing into the shore. As the aircraft traveled 80 to 100 mph and neared the top of the large waves, the right wing tip touched first, hitting a high wave, causing the *Polecat* to turn sharply clockwise and cartwheel into the water. This high impact contact with the North Sea was violent and bounced Fred hard around the cockpit, fatally injuring him. Pilots only had on seat belts, not the restraining harnesses used today. The old warrior B-17F *Polecat* finally came to rest and immediately began taking on water through the shattered open bomb bays and side windows and settled and sunk into the North Sea.

Fred's plans were to climb through the side cockpit window and swim to shore in the freezing sea. However, due to the one-thousand-foot distance to the beach and with one arm wounded and water temperatures hovering just above freezing, it was virtually impossible that he could make it even if he had survived the crash.

Knowing how much he loved his beautiful and loving wife Geri, there is no doubt she was also on his mind in those final moments. Geri had faithfully written to Fred every single day since he departed the United States, but sadly, those letters had never been delivered to Fred.

Large waves from high winds 15-25 mph crashing into the North Sea Texel beach at Paal 19, where the *Polecat* piloted by Lt. Fred Delbern and Lt. Don Neff came down on December 16, 1943 (Photo credit M. I. Darter)

The *Polecat's* twenty-second and last combat mission over Europe was over. She had completed twenty-two dangerous combat missions over

Europe, but this time, the *Polecat's* luck ran out. The aircraft hit hard, throwing Fred and unconscious Don around in the cockpit, knocking Fred unconscious. The aircraft sunk within two minutes with the large waves and wide open bomb bay doors and windows at 1404 (or 2:04 p.m.) as recorded and observed by Hptm. Grislawski watching overhead through the hole in the clouds. Grislawski claimed the kill for himself although he had nothing to do with it.

Cees Bonne and Michele Binsbergen who were children standing in the village heard the terrifying roar of the low-flying, smoking bomber over their tiny village. German soldiers quickly pulled out their guns and shot at the plane as it quickly roared just over the rooftops. The aircraft was so low it had to climb to just barely make it over the highest row of dunes between the village and the sea. The soldiers ran to the top of the dunes to see the crash site out in the North Sea just off the beach and to capture any crew who may have survived. But no one came out of the rapidly sinking aircraft. German interrogators later told Charlie in Frankfurt that two bodies were found in the plane, so they must have sent a diver down to check out the aircraft.

Had Fred decided to fly on toward England, there is no doubt that Hptm. Grislawski would have dived down and blasted the *Polecat* to pieces. Or would he? A recent book by Adam Makos tells the amazing story that occurred just four days after this mission where an American B-17 bomber, *Ye Old Pub*, which was also badly damaged over Bremen and straggling back toward the North Sea with no escort protection or even crew gunners inside was spotted by another German ace, Franz Stigler, who needed only one more kill to claim his Knight's Cross (the highest honor a German pilot could receive).

But as he flew his ME109 closer to the B17, he noted it was severely damaged and the remaining crew was huddled in the plane with no guns pointing at him. Stigler flew right up on the wing tip to see a shocked American pilot, Lt. Charlie Brown, in the cockpit. The German ace, sensing the helplessness of the crew and realizing that the German flak batteries were just ahead and ready to destroy the B-17, amazingly flew along just three feet from the right wing tip of the badly shattered B17, leading it directly over a very confused German flak battery that decided not to fire at the last second and directly out into the North Sea on their way back to England, literally saving the lives of the surviving crew.

Stigler then waved and saluted the American pilot and flew off back to Germany. The book is called *A Higher Call* and recounts this amazing act of chivalry. Many years later, the American pilot located the German pilot and the two, plus the survivors of the American crew had an amazing emotional reunion. The American crew wept in gratitude that the German pilot had saved their lives.

Given this shocking event, it begs the question: what would Lt. Alfred Grislawski have done had he also flew up to the shattered *Polecat* and noticed no crew except the pilot and the dead copilot in the cockpit? We will never know the answer.

1404 Hours: The Wreckage of the B-17F Lonesome Polecat II Rests Shattered on the Seabed in Many Pieces

The German soldiers ran to the top of the dunes just in time to see the *Polecat* sink below the tops of the waves and witnessed that no crew got out of her. So that they could document what happened to each of the crew, divers were dispatched to determine how many crew were in the aircraft. They reported that two bodies were all that were on board, which was entered into the German record and reported to the crew during interrogation later. The location of the crash site of the *Polecat* and the fate of the two pilots has been on the minds of the former crew members for the past sixty years. Year after year, evidence has accumulated to locate the crash site.

German Fighter Claims

As mentioned, high above the Wadden Sea and the *Polecat* was one of Germany's top aces, Hptm. Alfored Grislawski. He had followed the straggling, smoking American B17 for some time, waiting for the American escort P-47s to depart so that he could easily finish off the straggling Flying Fortress. He noted the parachutes coming out of the bomber near or over Texel Island, had radioed their location to the German HQ on Texel, and wondered what the pilots would do. Would they bail out, make a run for England, or ditch in the North Sea? A document entitled O. K. L. Fighter Claims, Reich and Western Front, 1943, included the following two claims by German pilots for December 16, 1943 (Film C. 2031/Il Anerk: Nr.10 and 11)[38]:

- Hptm. Alfored Grislawski: 117, B-17, off De Koog: Texel. 1404.
- Lt. Martin Lacha: 18, B-17, off De Koog: Texel. 1404.

Note the location and time that both German pilots saw a B-17 crash "off De Koog, Texel," at the same time: 1404 (or 2:04 p.m.). The operational records for the Bremen mission on December 16, 1943, indicate no other B-17s were lost near Texel on that day.

Thus, this evidence (along with the eyewitnesses on the ground in De Koog village) is conclusive and establishes that the crash site was "just off" the village of De Koog, which matches closely with Paal 19. When this German record was found, Johan Grass also located information on Hptm. Grislawski, who was one of Germany's top aces, credited with 132 shoot downs, one of which was the *Polecat*. Grislawski survived the war and died in 2003.

German Interrogator Statement

The German interrogating officers in Frankfort told each of the crew members that their aircraft crashed in the North Sea. The brief statement written by Charles Schreiner in his MACR stated, "Germans said they found the ship and found 2 bodies in it,"[3] and Charlie also stated the exact same thing in his letter to Mrs. Delbern in November 1945.[36] This tends to indicate the aircraft was in relatively shallow water, so divers could go down and examine the wreckage during wintertime.

Diary of Mr. K. Kok

During Johan Graas and my first visit to Texel on September 29, 2000, we met a long-term Texel resident, Mr. Bakker, in Den Berg. Mr. Bakker has the original diary of a former resident of Texel Island, Mr. K. Kok. He was an inhabitant of Texel during the war and was in the area of the dunes near De Koog village on the afternoon of December 16, 1943. Mr. Kok has since died, but here is a translated excerpt from his diary for December 16, 1943[29]:

> *Directly in the beginning of the afternoon many aircrafts where coming over. I hear one aircraft crashed into sea. [Note: No other*

*known Allied or German aircraft crashed in the Texel are a on
this afternoon.]*

*Crewmembers came down in Eierland. [Note: an area of
Texel Island was called Eierland, which was northeast of De Koog
and was on the flight path of the Polecat in the area where four
crew including Charlie, Doral, Frank, and Bob landed.]*

*It was impossible to see anything due to very heavy fog, but I
hear the sounds very good. [Note: The crash must have been close
to the shore to hear this well.]*[29]

This diary excerpt is indeed remarkable and valuable and gave
me great hope as it helps to establish the crash site of the *Polecat* and
identifies the general location of the crew members that landed on the
island. It also establishes that the stricken aircraft crashed near the Texel
shore as Mr. Kok "heard the sounds very good" despite the heavy fog.
The timing of the crash in the beginning of the afternoon agrees with the
time recorded by the two German pilots (1404 hours).

Eyewitnesses in De Koog Village

In early September of 2002, my son Paul Darter and I made another
visit to Texel and wrote another article for the *Texelse Courier* newspaper,
asking for help for possible eyewitnesses. A few days after we returned,
Mr. Cees Bonnie wrote an e-mail and Mr. Michele Binsbergen a letter
providing the most amazing and important information obtained
thus far.

*Cees Bonne: I lived then in the farm that with the name "The
Kuip" in De Koog. Now it is disco De Metro (a disco located on
the main village street in De Koog). I was six years old, but I can
still recall it very good. I was standing with my father and brother
near by the farm when the plane approached. I now am almost
certain that German soldiers were shooting at it with their guns.
It was indeed the left inside motor that was standing still (#3).
Near to my knowledge was also another motor turning very slow
(probably #2 windmilling).*

*The plane came very low over the farm; it had to climb to get
over the dunes, because it had still two working motors left. The*

incredible of my story, and sometimes even myself doubt at it: by the motor that was standing still sat a crewmember on the wing! The plane passed that low that I dare to swear that it happened like this, despite me being a very small boy. But I can still recall it very good.[31]

Michele Binsbergen: *From Cees and Will Bonne I got a copy of your e-mail dating Sep. 7, 2002 because I sent a reaction on Cees' column in our local newspaper: I also saw the B-17! I was standing on the other side of the street at only approximately 60 yards distance from the position where Cees and his dad were standing. On that morning (I cannot remember the date, but I was 12 years old) I ran out of the house attracted by the roaring sound of engines; it was nearly frightening and I had never before seen a plane so low, so nearby! There I stood perplexed between our house and hotel "de Toekomst" (the Future) amidst some German soldiers and Caucasians (Chechens and Dagestani: soviet POWs who joined the Wehrmacht to save their lives). They started shooting with their rifles: a doubtful attempt and I laughed at them . . . It all went rather quickly, the plane passed in seconds. From my position close to the hotel building I was looking at a sharp angle and could not see the person on the right hand wing . . .*

Some of the Germans walked quickly to the top of the Badweg (large grass and brush covered sand dunes), no-go area for us, they came back afterwards and shouted "Er ist gefallen" (it went down) in a way that the crash was a result of their shooting. (In those days we tended to believe it was the common German propaganda, because there was no sound of a crash.)[32]

Mr. Binsbergen also provided some answers to questions:

When the plane kept its steady course it would have crashed between beach marker (Paal) 20 and 19, but it can be possible that for an emergency landing a course correction could have been preferred to come down in shallower water; in that case "near" Paal 19 is more correct, but this is guessing. I heard no crash; there are two lines of dunes between beach and village. (Note: There exist quite high dunes about two hundred feet that would make it difficult to hear any crash.)[32]

These men indicated that the B-17F passed just south of the intersection of Badweg and Dorpsstraat streets in the center of De Koog village. The photo below shows an aerial view of the village of De Koog on the far right and the large dunes in the center and the beach along the North Sea on the far left. The *Polecat* flew just over the rooftops of De Koog (searching desperately for a place to make an emergency landing) and then, sighting the row of high dunes ahead through the fog, had to climb to get over the dunes just north of the current Opduin Hotel. Then as the aircraft crossed the two rows of dunes, it turned sharply to the left and was brought down quickly and crashed approximately one thousand feet off the beach in the North Sea near beach marker (Paal) #19.

Overview of the B-17F *Polecat* flying low over De Koog village, climbing over the high dunes, turning sharply to the left, and crashing into the North Sea (Image credit Google Earth)

Both Bonne and Binsbergen told me that the aircraft was so low over the rooftops that it had to climb to barely skim over the high ridges of dunes before reaching the beach and the North Sea. The ability of Fred to pull back on the stick to quickly bring up the nose of the severely damaged *Polecat*, given his injuries, shows just how skilled he was as a pilot. The German soldiers ran to the top of the second row of dunes and reported that "it went down" as if they had shot it down. They watched to see if anyone came out of the aircraft and would have captured them as they swam to the shore. Cees Bonne's comment about a crew member sitting on the wing is quite interesting, but it would be impossible for a crew member to climb out onto a B-17 wing in flight. He probably saw the feathered #3 engine props, which looked very odd on a flying aircraft.

Illustration of the *Polecat* with the #2 engine smoking badly as it roared over the roofs of De Koog village near the North Sea (Photo credit M. I. Darter)

CHAPTER 15

RECENT DISCOVERIES OF THE B-17F *POLECAT*

Lost Nets of Fishing Boat, 1981 and 1984

The waters around Texel are fished extensively, and fishermen have occasionally lost their fishing nets on ship and aircraft wrecks off the shores of Texel Island ever since the end of the war. This can be a large economic loss to a fisherman, and thus, they have been locating wrecks on maps and bringing up parts of downed aircrafts for years to clear the waters. Until the early 1980s, there was no known aircraft wreck in the North Sea identified near the North Sea village of De Koog, Texel, even though this is where the *Polecat* was observed to crash.

In 1981, Hans Eelman was contacted by a fisherman who had snagged and damaged his nets on a large wreck off the North Sea beach near De Koog. Hans was born in De Koog, Texel, and is a diver, a fisherman, and a man of many talents, living his entire life on Texel. In both 1981 and 1984, fishermen told Hans about losing their nets on a wreck in the North Sea just three hundred meters (one thousand feet) off the shore at beach marker Paal 19. Mr. Sief Boom (captain of old TX 50) told Hans in November 1981 that he had torn his fishing nets on both sides of his boat on a wreck at Paal 19 just offshore near De Koog. The nets which hang on booms on both sides of the fishing boat were damaged, which included a width of about 131 feet (forty meters). Hans concluded that the wreckage below was a large wreck. A B-17 is seventy-four-foot long and has a 104-foot wingspan. Hans believes that this was a large aircraft wreckage to catch nets over that width. Hans put an *X* on his Texel map to mark the site. The depth of the water at that location was noted to be only about ten feet (three meters). In 2001, Johan Graas asked Hans about information regarding a B-17 wreckage near De Koog, and Hans gave Johan a copy of his map that showed the following:

o *X* for the wreckage location about three hundred meters (one thousand feet) offshore
o 3 +/- meters (ten feet) depth of water
o Nets caught on both sides of the fishing vessel, large wide wreckage (e.g., aircraft)
o Approximate location in the North Sea:
  • 53 degrees, 5.9 minutes.
  • 4 degrees, 44.7 minutes.
  • Google Earth was used to find this location, and it checked out to be approximately three hundred meters out from Paal 19 (53.0983, 4.7450).

Then in 1984, Texel boat TX10 caught some nets on a wreck near Paal 19, and this was also reported to Hans. Alfonos Boom, brother of Sief, was captain of this boat TX 10, which is still a working fishing boat today in Texel harbor.

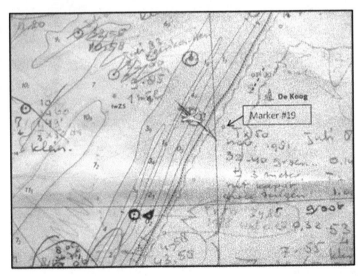

Map of the crash site of the B-17F (#42-30255) *Lonesome Polecat II* near the village of De Koog, beach marker #19, approximately three hundred meters or one thousand feet off the beach, as located by two Texel fishing boats in November 1981 and 1984[30,48] (Map credit Hans Eelman, Texel, NL)

The Texel North Sea shore erodes quickly in major storms and has been actively shored up by the Dutch government for many years by blowing sand (obtained far out in the North Sea) along the beach from a large ship. I have often watched ships blow sand into the sea out about one thousand feet from the beach. This effort has clearly covered over the aircraft wreckage field with lots of sand.

A Remarkable Pilot and Man

Lt. Fred Delbern died in the stricken *Polecat* as it crashed into the sea. German soldiers ran to the top of the dunes overlooking the North Sea and watched the aircraft as it sunk into the sea. Had Fred or Don escaped from the cockpit and swam ashore, the soldiers would have been waiting for them, and they would have been taken to the same location as the four other crew and perhaps given medical treatment and become POWs. Thus, it is believed that both of their remains are still in the sunken aircraft, which has now been covered over by several feet of sand.

Just a month previous, the *Polecat*, with Lt. John Miller at the controls, had faced a very similar situation over Bremen and miraculously made it back as described in chapter 2. But this second all-out attempt at fate to return to their base at Horham had fallen short, and they were unable to save their lives by ditching the aircraft. But they did indeed make a valiant and successful attempt to save the lives of their crew with one exception.

Loren Dodson, top turret and flight engineer, stated the following about Fred Delbern:

> We were lucky to have Fred Delbern for a pilot. He loved those big awkward B-17 planes, and he was at the height of his glory when he was at the controls. He wasn't overbearing or demanding, yet he expected the best from each member of the crew. He believed each member had the ability to perform their duties without having to be driven to perform them. He cared very much for his crew, and he was always looking for ways to make our lives a little more comfortable as well as better. If he saw an opportunity to get us a

*promotion he would do it. He asked me several times about our
food and living conditions; were we getting enough to eat, was the
food good, was our barracks comfortable? He would always say,
"Tell me the truth, don't lie to me, if they are not right we will get
them right." All the crew had the greatest respect for him and was
glad to have him for our pilot.*[2]

Charlie Schreiner gave his feelings about Fred Delbern in a letter to
Fred's wife:

*Our entire crew was strongly attached to Freddie. Each man in the
crew admired, respected and loved Fred in a man's way. In all the
time I knew him, only once did I ever draw an angry word from
him. Possibly you remember the time we argued in that Spokane
Hotel-Café. You were there.*

   *Del always treated every man in the crew equally and with
consideration. As a plane commander he could not be beat and
as a pilot he was aces. Us guys should know because we lived and
breathed flying together. Del' often said to other pilots that he
felt plenty lucky that he had a crew of competent men. When the
showdown came, we gave our best. Personally, I feel confident
every man in our crew was qualified to carry his job through to the
end without question or hesitation. Our ten men fought splendidly
as a team and I am proud that I had the privilege to fight side
by side with such swell guys. Under desperate combat conditions
you find exactly what men are made of—and that is why I feel as
strongly as I do about my crewmates.*[46]

The Legendary B-17

A total of 12,731 B-17s were produced. Eugene Fletcher, a pilot in the
95th BG who flew thirty-five missions, stated that the legendary B-17
was capable of "absorbing tremendous damage during combat and still
bringing its crew safely home."[7] After the war, Fletcher met the B-17
designer Ed Wells and stated that Wells must have followed Murphy's law,
"If anything can possibly go wrong . . . it will, so design accordingly."[7]
However, the *Lonesome Polecat II*, after twenty-one dangerous missions

and near disasters finally ran out of luck on this, her twenty-second combat mission.

Lonesome Polecat?

On a lighter note, just where did the name *Lonesome Polecat* come from? I met Mr. Arthur Watson, who was at Horham from 1943-45 (he had received the Legion of Merit for correcting a serious problem on the electronic supercharger control system on the B-17), at a reunion of the 95th BG. Art actually remembered the *Lonesome Polecat II* B-17F and the nose art on the aircraft as the aircraft flew many missions from Horham from June to December 1943 when he was on the base.[22] The name and art came from the Lil' Abner cartoon, which was very popular for many years. The Lonesome Polecat was a Native American cartoon character known to all these men. The 1940 *Lil' Abner* movie had a Native American played by Buster Keaton, the Lonesome Polecat. There was also a song from the movie musical *Seven Brides for Seven Brothers* called the "Lonesome Polecat." "I'm a Lonesome Polecat, lonesome sad and blue, 'cause I ain't got no feminine polecat vowing to be true."

Just below is the only known photo of the actual *Lonesome Polecat II* B-17F on a damage report dated July 4, 1943, on a mission to La Pallice, France, detailing the damage caused by a .5-caliber case that came from a B-17 in front of the *Lonesome Polecat II* (#42-30255). (The case was deflected by one of the propellers of the *Lonesome Polecat II* into the Plexiglas nose cone. An aircraft repairman can be seen in the nose cone.)

A photo of the crash site just off the beautiful Texel beach (#19) is shown below. I was taken out by a small boat to the area where the map indicates the *Lonesome Polecat II* rests by Gerrit Betsema of Texel. It was quite an emotional experience to be just above the old aircraft within which lie the remains of the two brave pilots buried under the sand forever more. Looking back at the shore, the location of the aircraft is a very long distance that would have made it extremely difficult for either pilot to swim the distance in the very cold, near-freezing temperatures on that day, especially in their injured condition. I doubt very much if Fred could have made it even if he was not injured given the experience of Harold Kious in chapter 12. Pilot Fred Delbern and copilot Don Neff did their best to return the *Lonesome Polecat II* entrusted to them to their base at Horham, England, while severely injured.

Only photograph of actual *Lonesome Polecat II* nose cone (B-17F #230255).
Note hole in Plexiglas nose cone caused by shell casing.
(Photo credit United States Army Air Corps)

North Sea beach at about beach marker 19 near De Koog village where the *Polecat* B-17F lies about one thousand feet out under ten feet of water and perhaps ten feet more of sand. The remains of pilot Lt. Fred Delbern and copilot Lt. Don Neff remain in the aircraft. These wounded pilots flew the severely damaged B-17F 166 miles from Bremen, Germany, and saved the lives of seven of the crew. (Photo credit M. I. Darter)

Continuing Search for B-17F Lonesome Polecat II

Hans Eelman was first made aware of a large wreckage near beach marker Paal 19 in November 1981 and again in 1984 by fishermen who lost their nets on the wreckage. Since that time, the wreckage has become covered by sand dredged out further in the North Sea and brought by ship to the Texel beach to shore up the constant erosion from North Sea storms.

At my request, Hans was very kind to perform a major sonar scan of the North Sea bottom area around beach marker 19 in August 2012. The map below was prepared by Hans, showing the area and grid over which he conducted a sonar scan in an attempt to locate the wreckage. However, nothing of significance was located in the grid area. Hans believes that the aircraft may have settled deeper into the sand and/or the years of dumping of sand over the wreckage to "shore" up the beach may have covered it over, making it impossible to locate with sonar technology. Other technology called magnetic profiling may be used next to try and locate the wreckage, as the four large engines are pretty hard to hide from a magnetic profile.

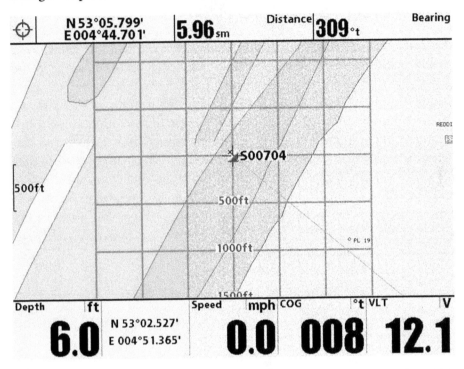

Sonar scan conducted by Hans Eelman of Texel, Netherlands (2012). The grid is five hundred feet square and in the north/south and east/west directions. Note: (1) Yellow color is the beach area of Texel Island, and green and the subsequent blue represent deeper and deeper North Sea water offshore at marker Paal 19, which is shown as an open circle PL 19. (Map image Hans Eelman, Texel, NL)

What Might Have Happened to the Polecat (A Current Experience with Engine Fire, Chicago, June 13, 2011)

The *Polecat's* engine #2 was hit by enemy fighters thirty to forty miles west of Bremen and was on fire and badly smoking for nearly forty minutes and 136 miles to Texel Island when Lt. Delbern ditched in the North Sea just off De Koog. All along the route, several crew expressed fear and concern over the black smoke coming from the engine (which indicated an oil fire). They had heard about many B-17s that had simply blown up in the air when a fire occurred in an engine, including the one described in chapter 5. This B-17 was from the 95th BG named Roger the Lodger (see photo with fuel fire behind the #2 engine) just moments before it exploded and fell into the North Sea.

Recently, on June 13, 2011, a B-17 known as the *Liberty Belle* took off from Aurora, Illinois, airport (near Chicago), and the crew soon noticed a fire in one engine. The pilot immediately brought the plane down and made an emergency landing in a plowed field, and all seven people on board got out and survived without injury. The aircraft, however, burned up in the field because the firefighters' trucks could not reach the burning plane due to the wet and soft soil. The crash site was about five miles from takeoff at Aurora airport. This current-day disaster illustrates the high risk and danger of any type of fire on an airplane and the speed at which it can get out of control. The *Polecat* crew was extremely fortunate their plane did not blow up, killing all of them in the air, as so many did during the war. The *Polecat* was fortunate indeed to have survived this far on the flight back to England.

CHAPTER 16

INTERROGATION REPORTS ON THE COMBAT MISSION

This chapter was mostly extracted directly from the 95th BG operations record for December 16, 1943, which is a packet of information of over two hundred pages obtained from the National Archives.[4] Information in parentheses was added. In addition, two newspaper accounts of the raid are provided at the end of the chapter. The text describes the dangerous aerial war over the skies of Europe that the young airmen were subjected to and many not returning nearly every day.

Units Taking Part in Bremen Raid

A total of 631 aircraft took part in the raid on December 16, 1943, to Bremen, Germany. These consisted of the following units: 94th, 95th (lost one B-17, the *Lonesome Polecat II*), 96th (lost seven B-17s), 100th, 385th, 388th, 390th (lost one B-17), 44th, 93rd, 389th, 392nd, 445th, 446th, 91st, 92nd (lost one B-17), 303rd, 305th, 306th, 351st, 379th, 381st, 384th, 401st, and 482nd. The 95th was the second group over the target on this day, and the German antiaircraft gunners were already in full operation with black flak explosions filling sky.

A total of ten B-17s were lost, with 104 crewmen missing (ten crewmen were from the *Polecat*). The attack was made between 1309 and 1322 hours at altitudes of 22,000 to 27,000 feet.

Base Engineering Report on Combat Mission

The main 95th BG (A and B formations) continued on the planned flight path from Bremen to Texel Island. They crossed the Dutch coast in Texel at 1358 (A Group) and 1359 (B Group). Note that the average ground speed of the main formation was approximately 203 mph as calculated by dividing the time from Bremen (1310) to Texel (1359) by 166 miles. The English coast was reached at 1434 hours just north of Lowestoft.

Forty B-17F airplanes of the 95th BG took off as per schedule, and thirty-two B-17F airplanes returned to base after completion of the mission. Eight planes did not return to base. Seven of these planes landed at other bases in England, and #230255 (*Lonesome Polecat II*) was lost and never located.

A Group: Eighteen B-17s plus one PFF took off at 0855 hours to bomb Bremen, Germany. All planes bombed the target and returned to base at 1635, except plane #3263, which landed rather badly damaged at Bungay, England. After losing two engines, this plane had a mild midair collision with A/C #7894, which was able to continue to the base. This group sustained no injuries to personnel, but the above two A/C were rather seriously damaged, and four others reported slight battle damage.

This group encountered ten to twenty enemy aircraft (E/A), chiefly FW 190s, just after leaving the target. These made attacks, which were not particularly aggressive, but it is believed that they destroyed or damaged five E/A. Clouds prevented appraisal of bomb damage, but its believed target area was well hit. *No fighter escort was received on route to target, but P-47s met formations ten to fifteen minutes after leaving target.* (Note that this timely arrival of the P-47s saved the *Polecat* and its crew from immediate destruction because the enemy aircraft would have finished her off in one more attack.)

B Group (including the Lonesome Polecat II): Twenty-two A/C took off beginning at 0835 to attack Bremen, Germany. These planes made up the 95th BG B Group. Twenty A/C attacked, with two A/C returning early. Twenty A/C dropped on the lead PFF (pathfinder aircraft) with apparently good results as much black smoke was seen billowing through the undercast in the target area. The flak was intense and of a following barrage type over the target. Other flak of meager intensity and inaccurate was encountered from Cuxhaven, Alfastedt, and Texel Island.

Ten to fifteen E/A, FW 190s, and ME 109s attacked this formation, concentrating on tail attacks on the low squadron (i.e., the *Lonesome Polecat II*). The high squadron experienced one frontal attack by five ME 109s in trail and one overhead attack by three ME 109s.

Aircraft #230255 is missing (the Lonesome Polecat II). It was seen to leave the formation with #3 engine out just before target but continued on to drop bombs on target and then fell back. E/A attacked this ship west of target, and three chutes came out. A/C was last seen ten minutes from target, disappearing into clouds but still under control.

Four A/C landed at other fields, and three men were wounded in all other ships and returned to base by 1615 hours.

Flak Report: Intense and accurate fire from Bremen, with two box barrages on either side of course, with much continuous following fire on course.

Only one plane missing: #230255 (Lonesome Polecat II). No other men missing. Zero wounded in the A Group and three wounded in the B group. Group A reported three enemy A/C destroyed, one probably, and one damaged. Group B reported nine enemy A/C destroyed, two probably, zero damaged. Note that the crew of the *Polecat* believes they shot down five enemy aircraft. The *Polecat* was far below the Group A and B formation when all of these attacks were occurring.

Results of the Raid on Bremen

Although clouds prevented any damage assessment, strike photographs show heavy black smoke rising above the target area to a height of over seven thousand feet after the attack. Some information obtained from the 95th BG operations record for December 16, 1943, is included as follows:

> *The bombers were escorted over enemy territory by P-47's, P-38's and P-51's of the VIII Fighter Command* (apparently the 4th, 355th and 356th Fighter groups). *Ten B-17's were lost due to either flak or enemy aircraft. Claims for enemy aircraft are 18 destroyed, 11 probably destroyed, and 11 damaged* (this mission was one of the very first with P-51 escorts).
>
> *Few rockets were used. An FW-190 was seen to drop what appeared to be a 4 by 4-metal net on a B-17, with no visible*

results. An enemy aircraft was observed towing a small object about 100 yards behind it. The AC then dipped sharply over a B-17, the No. 2 engine of which soon afterward burst into flames. This appears to have been a cable-bomb attack (could this have been the Lonesome Polecat II since its #2 engine was set aflame also during the aerial battle?).

Six crewmembers were killed, 3 were seriously wounded, 2 were slightly wounded and 104 are missing. 10 B-17's were lost, 8 to E/A and 2 from unknown causes.

The following information was obtained from a later document titled Determination of Status under Public Law 490, dated December 17, 1944, stating the following: *The status of 45 members of the crews of 8 planes lost in the Bremen raid on 16 December 1943 is the subject of this review. Thirty-five of the eighty men have been accounted for—26 are dead and nine are POW.*

Fighter escort: Penetration, target and withdrawal escort was provided by 3 groups of P-47's, 1 group of P-38's, and 1 group of P-51's. Adverse weather again hindered location of bombers by our fighters.

S-1 report:

Attacks took place between the target and point when fighter escort picked up formation, which was approximately 15 minutes beyond target (1325). (This arrival just in time saved the *Lonesome Polecat II* from certain destruction.)

First E/A encountered about 1315, just after target, and lasted about 15 minutes (1330).

Twenty to fifteen E/A were seen, which were predominately FW190's, and ME 109's. One JU88 was encountered. Ten to fifteen E/As were encountered by this group.

The low squadron of this group was attacked quite heavily from the tail, although a few attacks were made on the high squadron. In one instance 5 ME 109's abreast attacked the tail of the low squadron, dived below and climbed back to make a frontal attack, in tax trail, on the high squadron. The high squadron also reports three E/A attack from almost overhead at 1 o'clock.

One B-17 is missing from Group B: A/C No. 230255. A/C had No. 3 engine out but was apparently under control. A/C dropped out of formation over the target and was last seen 10 minutes west of target disappearing into clouds. A/C #230255 was last seen about 1320 with three chutes from it. (This is the *Lonesome Polecat II*, with Jackson, Woollen, and Dodson bailing out near Oldenburg and Leer, Germany.)

Bomber Losses from All Groups

Ten B-17s were reported missing after the raid. The *Lonesome Polecat II*, however, was the only one lost from the 95th BG that day. Two tragic collisions occurred between planes from other groups. Both Charlie Schreiner and Doral Hupp recall seeing some of these occur. Here are notes from the 95th BG operations record for December 16, 1943.

> *95th BG: A/C 230255 (Lonesome Polecat II) was observed 10 minutes west of target disappearing into clouds with No. 3 engine out but apparently under control. Last seen about 1320 hours with three chutes coming from it.*
>
> *Ninety-Sixth A: Two B-17s collided at 1408 hours after fighter attack and went down at 5393N-0440E. No chutes were seen.*
>
> *Ninety-Sixth B: Two B-17s collided after fighter attack and went down at 53 07N-05 12E. Last seen going down in a tight spin at 1352 hours. No chutes seen.*
>
> Note: The 95th BG was just behind the 96th BG and one 95th BG pilot told me that they saw one of these two sets of B-17s collide vertically and stick together, unable to separate, and went down together with no crew seen to get out alive.

Three other B-17s blew up under fighter attack.

Complete cloud cover at target. Many crews reported black smoke billowing up through clouds after leaving target ("After leaving target saw lots of black smoke came through 10/10ths").

The German defense of Bremen was strong and determined, trying as hard as they could to force the Americans to end the daylight bombing of Germany.

Two newspaper accounts of the Bremen mission on December 16, 1943, follow.

USAAF Strikes Home of Big FW Factories and Submarine Pens

Flying Fortresses of the Eighth Air Force struck in force yesterday at Bremen, great North Sea port which harbors Germany's long-range U-boats and industrial center which includes the biggest of the Focke-Wulf assembling plants.

The bombers, escorted part of the way by Thunderbolts, delivered the third American daylight blow at the port this year. At a late hour last night no further details of the mission had been announced by Eighth Air Force headquarters. German news agency said: "In the center of Bremen there was large-scale destruction in residential quarters and damage was done to public buildings and cultural monuments." In the American raid, though no details were available officially last night, it was reported that the Fortresses and P47 escorts shot down a large number of enemy interceptors.

Returning crewmen said the flak encountered over Bremen was some of the heaviest yet experienced. Berlin radio last night admitted that considerable damage was caused in the Fortress raid on Bremen.

Largest Force of Eighth Heavies Raids Bremen

56 Enemy Planes Down as Fighters Set Record; 29 Bombers Lost

The largest formations of Eighth Air Force heavy bombers ever dispatched from Britain bombed Bremen and operated over northern France Friday and left the great German inland port "well plastered" in spite of heavy anti-aircraft. Fifty-six enemy fighters were destroyed—36 of them by escorting Thunderbolts and Lightning's—for a new combat record. Twenty-nine heavy bombers, four mediums and five fighters were lost.

Bomber crews who went to Bremen, a major shipbuilding port which is the largest producer of 750 and 1,200-ton Nazi submarines, reported good bombing results, but one force of

Fortresses which went to France found its target covered by clouds and returned without dropping bombs. A standing order forbids indiscriminate bombing in the occupied countries.

In spite of Lightning and Thunderbolt escort over the target, some of the Fortress and Liberator formations which struck at Bremen encountered persistent attacks by as many as 100 German fighter planes. The raiders met an intense ack-ack barrage over the target.

It was "colder than hell" flying over Germany. 2/Lt. Bayard T. G. Dudley, of Houston, Tex., copilot of Ritzy Ritz, said the thermometer in his cockpit "went down to 48 degrees below zero; then the needle hit the peg and started to bend."

Two ball turret doors ripped off in the wind. One of the gunners, Sgt. Charles S. Bullions, of Mount Lebanon, Pa., crawled up into the plane and rode as a passenger the rest of the way, but the other, Sgt. Robert Dearth, of Columbus, Ohio, stuck it out in his open turret, despite the subzero gale, until after the bombs were dropped. It was 19-year-old Dearth's first mission.

CHAPTER 17

PRISONER-OF-WAR CAMPS AND THE LONG MARCH

The Lucky Survivors

All of the crew members that bailed out (except Eugene Darter) were captured within a few hours. With the exception of Pete Jackson (who was hospitalized from his injuries to his eye when he was hit by flak as he bailed out of the aircraft), the enlisted men were transported over the next few weeks to the infamous Stalag 17B POW camp near Krems, Austria, and the officers to the Stalag Luft POW camp in Barth, Germany.

Loren Dodson, Doral Hupp, and Charlie Schreiner all relate that after their bailout and capture and various times of confinement, all of the crew members were shipped by train to Frankfurt, Germany, where on Christmas Eve 1943, all surviving crew members were reunited with the exception of Jackson (who was still hospitalized for his injuries). They all were surprised and very concerned that Darter did not show up and wondered what happened to him, as well as to Delbern and Neff and the *Lonesome Polecat II* (although German intelligence had told them at the interrogation that the aircraft crashed in the North Sea and two bodies were found in the sunken wreckage).

Here are Loren Dodson's recollections on the transit to POW Stalag 17B (probably similar to what the other crew members experienced):

The next morning a guard took me to the depot in Leer, where we caught a train to Oldenburg, Germany. We arrived there as people were going home from work. We rode for a long way on a streetcar on our way across town to an army base and then on to a train depot to go to Frankfort. At the depot were several men waiting, among them was Eddie Woollen! What a thrill to see someone you knew!

The people on the streetcar didn't pay any attention to me even though I had blood stains down the front on my jacket and heated suit; my face was shot up and one eye swollen almost shut and both eyes beginning to turn black. Maybe it was old stuff to them.

We were taken to Frankfort where we were put in solitary confinement. We were there for three days and it was here the interrogation officer told me all about myself: who I was, where I had been (in my training) and what I had done! He was the one who told me our plane had crashed in the North Sea.

Frankfort was a transit camp for prisoners who were captured. They were held here until they had enough men to make a shipment to a permanent camp. It was on Christmas Day, 1943 just before sundown they took me out in the railroad yard (I think there was about 160 of us) and loaded us in two boxcars to begin our journey to Krems, Austria. At that time we had no idea where we were going; just that were going somewhere.[2]

Loren goes on to describe his state of mind, likely shared by most of the other crew members:

It's impossible to describe our state of mind at this point; the fears and confusion, the uncertainty. The knowledge and feelings as to just what had happened to us was beginning to sink in. The uncertainty of what lay ahead mixed with what had happened to our crew made it very difficult for us. There was no way one could have prepared oneself for a situation of this kind so you knew you would have to deal with the problems that came on a day to day basis.[2]

The five enlisted men spent the next sixteen months in the infamous Stalag 17B POW camp. Doral Hupp and Loren Dodson bunked together during this time, and Frank Lee was in a bunk just above them. Bob McKeegan and Charlie Schreiner were in a different building. The two officers, Jackson and Woollen, were sent to Stalag Luft POW camp in Barth, Germany.

In the POW camps, the men suffered from their combat wounds, the lack of food, the lack of medical assistance, and the freezing temperatures in the winter, to say nothing of fear of being shot. Toward the end of their imprisonment, the men in Stalag 17B were forced to walk 260 miles across Austria to Braunau (Hitler's birthplace) to the Inn river—quite a physically and emotionally stressful experience. The following are the crew's experiences in Stalag 17B and the long march by Bob McKeegan, Frank Lee, Charlie Schreiner, Doral Hupp, and Loren Dodson.

Doral Hupp Recollections on Stalag 17B

Stalag 17B was a former Hitler Youth Camp. It was located about 3 or 4 miles by foot outside of Krems, Austria. The Danube River ran through Krems, which was located about 60 miles west from Vienna, and about 20 or 30 miles south from the Czech Republic border. The camp was formed in October 1943, and we arrived in January 1944. We left the camp on April 10, 1945, and were forced to travel by foot approximately 260 miles west across Austria to the Inn River at the border of Bavaria (Germany). Apparently, the Russian Army was closing in on the Stalag 17B POW camp. Patton's 3rd Army released us from the Germans on 5 May 1945. My brother was in the 3rd Army and came in to the camp looking for me, but I had left on the last flight to Camp Lucky Strike in France.[2]

Loren Dodson Recollections on Stalag 17-B

We arrived at Krems, Austria (near Vienna) on New Year's Eve, 1943. It was well after dark. Snow was on the ground and we had a 2.5 mile walk up the hill to the prison camp. Stalag 17-B. Hitler had built this camp in the middle 1930's to house political figures. They were rough tarpaper barracks with no heat in them. Krems was in the foothills of the Alps Mountains (about 90 miles from Vienna, Austria). There were lots of snow and lots of zero and sub-zero temperatures.

When we arrived in camp they herded us into an unheated room where we were told that they would have to delouse our clothes. They told us to remove all our clothes, they gave us big hooks to put them on, and then they were placed in the delouser. This process would take 3 hours. We were then taken to a shower room; our heads were sheared and then we were to take a shower. We were told to move fast as the water would be on for a very short time and if we got caught with soap on us it would be our hard luck. We were then taken back to the unheated room to wait for our clothes and we nearly froze. I took to a terrible cold and was sick for days.

We were taken to our barracks (this was around midnight), and each one was given two blankets (old, of course). One was fairly heavy and the other was very thin. Our bunks were double deck racks made from rough lumber; four men slept on each deck, two on one end and two on the other. The mattress was about a half inch thick (a bag with wood shavings in it; very cold and no padding). The fellows in the barracks told us we would have to sleep together in order to stay warm. They told us to put one of the heaver blankets under us to keep the cold from coming through the mattress and use the other three to cover up with. The Red Cross at Frankfort had given us Army overcoats and we used those also. Doral Hupp and I bunked together, and Frank Lee was on the upper deck with another fellow.

The food was terrible! The first winter they gave us turnips, rutabagas that are glorified turnips, and boiled potatoes with the peeling on them and a ration of a sour very black rye bread. There was boiled dehydrated cabbage that was full of little white worms, and then there was dehydrated potatoes which tasted very much like wallpaper paste. We were supposed to get a food parcel from the Red Cross each week but very few ever showed up. Some may have been lost in air raids, but I would rather think the Germans stole them.

The Gestapo would pull a shakedown once in a while, no real purpose in mind. Just an excuse to irritate and steal whatever they could get their hands on.

By Christmas of 1944 the food situation was getting critical. By that time the German railroads were either torn up so bad they couldn't move anything or they just didn't have it. We were getting four small potatoes you could hold in the palm of your hand plus a slice of that black rye bread. This was your food for the day.

Our favorite sport was watching the B-17's from the 9th Air Force fly over our camp headed for Venice and the area around there. But the greatest fun was when the P-38's would strafe and bomb Krems. They would fly over first outside the camp and dive behind some hills; then would come the sound of machine-gun fire, the sound of explosions. The planes would pop up over the hills for another run. The GI's would cheer and the guards would climb down out of the towers scared to death. This would make the GI's really cheer.

Krems was a major rail terminal as well as an oil field. So these raids were doing a lot of good.[2]

Loren Dodson Recollections on the Famous March

In the spring of 1945 the Russians were closing in on that area (Krems, Austria). The Germans decided they should move us to keep us from falling into their hands. This was really the only good thing they ever did for us. There were 4,000 Americans in the camp, and on Easter morning they divided us into groups of 500 and began our journey. The Germans felt the small groups would be much easier to handle than one large group. We headed west toward the Bavarian region. We went through the city of Linz, Hitler's old hangout. We would travel 2 days and rest a day.

We were on the road one morning when we saw a group of people approaching us from the other way. As we were coming together the Germans pushed the Americans to one side of the road and these people to the other side so we could all pass. These people were Jews, and I have never seen such a wretched looking group of people in my life. They were dirty, and their clothes were ragged, one patch on top of another. They were nothing but skin and bones, truly walking skeletons because they had been starved so long. They were yelling and screaming and leaning on each other for support as they struggled along. The Germans wouldn't allow the two groups to talk to each other if they could help it. After we passed, the highway behind them was covered with tattered blankets and clothing. They had carried them as far as they could; as far as their strength would permit. A little further down the road we saw a dead body lying in the road ditch; pretty soon another and then another. In what we estimated to be about a mile we counted thirteen bodies. These people had collapsed from weakness; the Germans had knocked them in the head with a rifle butt and rolled their bodies into the ditch. Some distance down the road we came to the Mauthausen Concentration Camp and apparently these people had come from there. Such are the horrors of war. [Note: Doral Hupp related the same experience above to M. Darter.]

We traveled about 2 weeks and covered 250 or 260 miles (traveling west across Austria), ending outside the City of Braunau in the Bavarian region. The German's had cleared a safety zone around a forest area, and they put us in this area with no shelter and very little to eat. We were here nearly 2 weeks. It was cold, cloudy, and it rained and even snowed one night. We had to gather pine-tree branches to fashion makeshift shelters. Some of the fellows were beginning to get really sick. It was decided to build a log cabin to serve as a shelter and hospital. A two-man crosscut saw was obtained, and guys who had some experience in that kind of work were appointed to oversee the project. I helped on that project, sawing the timbers. We were liberated before the project was completed![2]

Ed Woollen Recollections on the Stalag Luft POW Camp in Barth, Germany

Ed Woollen related the following information to his son, John Woollen, about his POW experience.

While a POW, the men were given very meager food rations. Sometimes a meal consisted only of some "potato-flavored water" and maybe a small piece of bread. When I asked him if they ever had meat to eat, he smiled and recalled one day they certainly did "when they managed to catch the old cat that had been prowling *around the compound." Dad's journal does note that arrival of Red Cross food packages were welcome breaks to the normally poor "Jerry rations."*

In his journal, Dad listed his serial number as ASN #0-746968. His POW number was #1891 at M-Stammlager Luft I, Barth Germany.

He recalled much time spent playing cards while a POW, to help pass the time and break the monotony. He said that from time to time the prisoners tried tunnels and other means to escape, but that almost all such attempts were discovered by the German guards.[24]

Royal (Pete) Jackson Recollections on the Stalag Luft POW Camp in Barth, Germany

Pete Jackson spent several months in a German hospital due to injuries to his eye. Eventually, he was sent to the Frankfort interrogation center and then to the POW camp, Luft 1, near Barth, Germany, where he was reunited with his crewmate Ed Woollen. His POW camp was near the runway at Barth, where the German ME-262 jets were stationed. He remembers them flying overhead. "The roar of the engines on takeoff was awesome." He said that at one time, a US P-47 flew in and destroyed a jet on the runway for which the men cheered wildly. They had a radio in the POW camp and knew the US was winning the war. He remembers large formations of B17s flying overhead on their way to Berlin and the cheering of the men (the 95th BG was on those missions in March 1944, being the first American unit to hit Berlin in the daylight).[2]

During these sixteen months of long fearful days and nights in prison, the crew discussed their mission and prayed for their three missing brothers that they may somehow somewhere still be alive.

CHAPTER 18

LIBERATION AND RETURN TO THE UNITED STATES, MINUS THE MIAS

L oren Dodson recalls that on the third day of May 1945 (after more than sixteen months of imprisonment), they began to hear gunfire:

We looked across the Inn River and saw American tanks moving about in the timber on that side. The German command decided their time had come and they made contact with tank commanders to come and liberate us. On the 3rd day of May 1945 a group from the 13th Armored Division came into camp to rescue us. It's impossible to describe the feeling as these men came into camp!

We were free at last! For us, the war was over!

We walked to the city of Braunau, where the 13th Armored Division was gathered for a short while before they continued on. This was about 4 to 5 miles. The sweetest and most enjoyable walk I've ever had. We were taken to an aluminum smelting plant, a huge place. It had been in production until the very end of the war as some of the furnaces were still warm.[2]

In a few days, the Air Force brought in C-47s and flew the ex-POWs to Camp Lucky Strike at Le Havre. They kept them there for military processing, physical exams, and General preparations to send them home, but they had to wait for several days for shipping. Amazingly, Doral

Hupp's brother was in the Third Army who came into the camp looking for him, but he had left on the last flight to Camp Lucky Strike at Le Havre, France.

The crew members were separated and did not get on the same ship or land in the same location in the US. Many of the crew members did not see each other again, but a few did keep in touch with each other over many years. They were all saddened to learn that there had been no sightings of their three crewmates Fred Delbern, Don Neff, and Eugene Darter.

Doral Hupp's Return Home

Doral Hupp stayed at Camp Lucky Strike about a week, being processed to return to the States. He left France on May 21 on a cargo ship called the *Marine Dragon*, and it took eleven days to reach Boston. From Boston, he was sent to a base outside of Indianapolis and later to Wright-Patterson Air Force Base, where he was discharged on October 29, 1945.

Loren Dodson's Return Home

After being at Camp Lucky Strike in France, we were finally loaded on ships one afternoon. We sailed across the English Channel to Southampton Harbor to stay overnight. On Memorial Day, 1945, we began our trip home.

We landed in New York Harbor on June 10th to a rousing welcome from boats of people who came out to welcome us. Men cried as they stood at the ship's rail and watched the Statue of Liberty come into view. What a beautiful Lady she was!

We were placed on trains and taken to Camp Kilmer to stay overnight and the next day on to Great Lakes Naval Station near Chicago. Here we were issued new clothes, given a partial payment and given orders for a 60-day furlough and then we were on our way home.[2]

Ed Woollen and Pete Jackson were liberated by Russian Forces on May 1, 1945. They left Barth by air (B-17s) for France on May 13,

1945, and arrived at Camp Lucky Strike on May 14. They left shortly thereafter for the United States and a happy homecoming. Pete stated that he was fortunate to come home on a destroyer that entered the New York harbor. After sixty years, Pete Jackson distinctly remembers seeing the Statue of Liberty and recalling what a thrill it was to him when tears of joy streamed down his face, thankful but realizing he would have only one eye the rest of his life.

Home at Last!

Loren no doubt expresses how all of the crew members felt when he says, "It seemed like heaven itself to see one's family, your friends and your home once again. It took days for this to sink in, to realize this was really true and not just a pleasant dream." They all had lost a lot of weight and were very skinny guys.

Bob McKeegan apparently arrived home very early in the morning and sat on his mother's porch until she awakened, and she was shocked to see him, but of course very happy!

Each crew member undoubtedly has a similar story to tell and experienced some very deep emotions when they arrived home. As time went on, the survivors communicated with each other at various times and also some with the wives and mothers and fathers of the three missing crew. They never forgot about their fallen brothers and that they were still missing and had not returned home. Each one that I met told me of their feelings of sadness and lack of closure for their fallen and still missing brothers. They longed to know of their fate.

And of course at this same time, the Darter, Delbern, and Neff families settled into further grief because their sons and husbands did not return with the other POWs. Where are they? What happened to them? How and where did they die?

CHAPTER 19

INVESTIGATIONS FOR MIAS

T hree crew members of the *Polecat* made the ultimate sacrifice of their lives on that fateful day of their first mission: Lt. Fred Delbern, Lt. Don Neff, and S/Sgt. Eugene Darter. Because the seven crew members were all captured within a few hours and rapidly transferred to the Stalag 17B POW camp (enlisted men) or the Luft 1 POW camp (officers) where they were interred for sixteen months and due to the ongoing war, there was no investigation into the location of the remains of these men until after the war ended. The German army heavily occupied Texel Island during the war, the shores were mined, and a brutal battle occurred on Texel just at the end of the war, so no search could be done until well after the end of the war.

Official US Military Investigation Reports

After the war ended in May 1945, due to the efforts of the relatives of Neff, Delbern, and Darter, there was an investigation to locate their remains. The Individual Deceased Personnel File (IDPF) for Eugene F. Darter was obtained from the Department of the Army, US Total Army Personnel Command.[1] This file contains many different documents, including the telegram to his parents announcing his missing in action, his medical and dental records, the aircraft engine serial numbers, and an American Graves Registration Command investigation in 1946-47 attempting to identify if any remains that were found in North

Holland were that of Darter, Neff, or Delbern. Brief summaries of the investigation are as follows:

Statement from the secretariat of the community of Texel in charge of the administration of war cemeteries dated November 18, 1947.[1]

1. All American victims buried in the War Cemetery at Den Berg, Texel, have been removed to American Cemeteries by the American Graves Registration Command. (According to a sign at the cemetery, they were removed to the Netherlands American Military Cemetery at Margraten.)
2. All unknown allied victims in the war cemetery have been disinterred by the British Graves Concentration Unit, and the bodies found to be those of Americans have also been transported to American Cemeteries.
3. That, as far as he knows, no American victims are buried on the island of Texel either in the War Cemetery at Den Burg or isolated.
4. That, as far as he knows, no planes crashed on the territory of Texel on 16 December 1943. (We now know that the *Lonesome Polecat II* crashed into the North Sea just 300 meters off the coast near the village of De Koog.)
5. Relatives of the American flyers Delbern, Neff, and Darter requested information from this town hall, but the town hall was not able to give any information.
6. That it is compulsory for the inhabitants of Texel to report any case of finding of a body etc., to this town hall.

Document entitled "Narrative" dated December 1, 1947 (Holland 8979).[1] This document states the following:

Investigation for the remains of S/Sgt Eugene F. Darter, 2nd Lt. Frederick A. Delbern, and 2nd Lt. Don P. Neff, proved negative.

Aircraft #230255 did not crash on the island of Texel the 16th of December 1943. Proof is given from the Town Hall's statement at Den Burg for the community of Texel Island. It is further stated that all military deceased buried at Den Burg have been disinterred by both the AGRC and the British GRU and those of American nationality were previously removed to a US Military Cemetery.

Checking at the Dutch War Department and the Dutch National Red Cross at The Hague, no further information concerning above-mentioned deceased could be found.

As aircraft #230255 did not crash on Texel Island it is therefore presumed to have crashed into the North Sea and unknowns recovered from this area cannot be associated with subject deceased. This gives cause to believe that the remains of Darter, Delbern, and Neff are unrecoverable.

Lloyd W. Bladow, US DA Civilian Investigator

Memorandum dated December 10, 1947, stating results of an investigation conducted in the Texel Island area for Delbern, Neff, and Darter.[1] This document states the following:

1. Investigation conducted in the Texel Island area failed to locate the remains of 2/LT Frederick A. Delbern, 2/Lt Don P. Neff, and S/Sgt Eugene F. Darter.
2. Interrogation of the civilian authorities in the above area failed to confirm the German Dulag Luft report that a B-17 type aircraft crashed on Texel Island 16 December 1943.
3. Unknowns identified as X-2118A, X-2118B, X-2002, X-2003, X-2004, X-2006, X-1942, X-1993, X-1998, X-1999, X-1930A, X-1930B, X-1948, X-2015, X-2700, X-4629, X-4432, X-4444, X-4632, X-3265, X-3266, X-4628, and X-4626 were recovered from the northern coastline of Holland and cannot be associated with the three missing crew of aircraft #230255.
4. Report of Investigation and attached statements pertaining to subject case area enclosed herewith.

Summary

Thus, an investigation was conducted and completed by the end of 1947. Comparisons were made between the three missing US airmen and twenty-three unknowns recovered along the northern coastline of Holland, and no match was found. The remains of these three men have never been located. However, it is clear that the German interrogators told some of the crew during the interrogation in Frankfort that two bodies (Delbern and Neff) were located in the sunken aircraft wreckage just off the coast of De Koog, Texel.

Some search was done by the Foundation for Aircraft Recovery 1940-45 (Holland), headed by Johan Graas, on the identification of any unknowns buried on any of the Frisian Islands and other cemeteries in North Holland and the Margraten American Military Cemetery where all identified American (known or unknown) were reburied after the war (there are 106 such unknowns buried in Margraten today, along with twenty-four unknowns buried at Cambridge). There are ten unknowns buried on Texel Island today, but none of these fit the timing of the *Lonesome Polecat II* crash.

The results of these investigations were only reported in General statements to the three families of the missing. The Darter family continued to hope and pray for the return of their son for decades to come. The surviving crew members never stopped thinking about their three comrades either and wanted to continue the investigation, but no more searching was done until January 2000 when this investigation began and continues until this day.

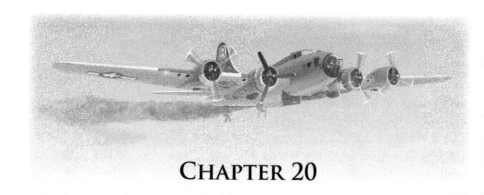

CHAPTER 20

HORHAM AIR BASE (STATION 119), ENGLAND TODAY

When I first arrived at the old airfield site in September 2000, nearly all of the original buildings had been removed, most of the airfield concrete pavements broken up and removed, and cultivated fields now existed. But from year to year as I returned to Horham airfield in search of further information about my brother, I witnessed an incredible revival of the once-dilapidated NCO's mess, the Red Feather Club, into a living museum of the 95th BG in WWII. This building was a key gathering point for the airmen and grounds crew throughout the war. Several impressive murals still exist that were painted on the walls by airman Nathan Brindler during the war.

One of several impressive seventy-year-old Red Feather Club painted murals (Photo credit M. I. Darter)

This remarkable restoration was accomplished over more than a decade by the 95th BG Heritage Association (UK), with help from the 95th BG Memorials Foundation in the US, to keep alive the memory of the 95th BG's role in WWII.[17] Led by James Mutton and a dedicated group of local people, literally hundreds of other volunteers donated thousands of hours of time to renovate and rebuild the Red Feather Club and to create a 95th BG museum of items exclusively used at the Horham base during the war.

The Red Feather Club now hosts regular 1940s dances, films, talks, educational visits from schools and other groups, and regular open days where hundreds attend, including former veterans of the 95th BG now in their late eighties and nineties. (Photo credit M. I. Darter)

Literally hundreds of local people have assisted in this incredible renovation and revival. There is now a fabulous 95th BG big band (just as there was during the war) that plays the great tunes of the forties and beyond, including Glenn Miller, who played one of his last concerts at the base before sadly becoming MIA himself over the English Channel. There is also the 95th BG Wallopers, an up-and-coming softball team on a steep learning curve, but who recently proved themselves by "walloping" an American team on Open Day 2013.

Those who early on worked hard on building the 95th BG Heritage Association and renovations included Frank Sherman, Alan Johnson,

John Blott, James and Christine Mutton, Norman Feltwell, and many others. When Frank Sherman was a boy of fifteen, he somehow got to take a flight in a B-17 bomber. He never forgot the thrill and has been very helpful in showing many veterans and families around the old Horham base area and was so helpful to me in explaining where my brother would have been on base as he prepared for his first combat mission and took off from the main Horham runway.

The old hospital building has also been privately restored and now contains a museum of many original artifacts of the WWII days. Fortunately, a proportion of the old main runway 25/07 remains. This is the primary runway where the 95th BG bombing missions departed beginning in June 1943. The remnants of two of the crosswind runways also remain. The remaining portion of the main runway 25/07 is occasionally used today by a private aircraft. My son Michael Olsen-Darter (nephew of S/Sgt. E. F. Darter) and I were given a special flight off the main runway that the *Polecat* and her brave crew took off on seventy years ago on their first bombing mission. As we raced down the old runway and lifted off into the "wild blue yonder," we thought about the *Polecat* crew and the feelings and thoughts that they must have had rolling down that runway toward the real war that was now upon them, never imaging what would befall them on their first combat mission over Germany.

Aerial photo of the old runway 25/07 with a white building constructed on the concrete pavement at the very end of the runway (the 07 end). This is the main runway where all heavily loaded B-17s once took off on so many dangerous missions over Europe. (Photo credit M. I. Darter)

Looking down the old main runway 25/07 on Horham Open House, June 2010, showing the flyover of the only B-17 in Europe called the Sally B. Hundreds of attendees and restored vehicles of World War II days were lined up on the old Horham main runway. A remarkable site and experience to hear the roar of a B-17 so close to us in the air! Both associations are working hard to keep the sacrifice of the men of the 95th BG alive. (Photo credit M. I. Darter)

The original ambulance used at Horham and also used in the 1990 movie *Memphis Belle*, the first B-17F crew to complete twenty-five missions in June 1943. Frank Sherman and (incredibly talented) artist John Blott are in the photo. John Blott produced the two paintings of the *Polecat* in this book based on detailed crew descriptions. (Photo credit M. I. Darter)

The tiny village of Horham is still there and just as beautiful as ever. St. Mary's Church is an ancient but beautiful building where some of the 95th

BG men worshipped. Times have changed, but memories remain forever of the life and death that took place at Horham, England, in WWII.

The 95th BG Memorial designed as the tail section of a B-17 is just across the church and is particularly fitting and impressive to the men who lived, flew, and died in the B-17s stationed at Horham (photo of several veterans of the Ninety-Firth, June 2013). (Photo credit M. I. Darter)

The plaque on the 95th BG Memorial in Horham states the following:

*In memory of the men of the
95th Bombardment Group who
served at Horham Airfield
and to those who gave their
lives in the cause of freedom.*

1943-1945

*334th, 335th, 336th, and 412th Bomb
Squadrons and supporting units.
Headquarters 13th Combat Bomb
Wing, United States 8th Air Force
Dedicated 18th Sept. 1981*

CHAPTER 21

TABLETS OF THE MISSING, X-FILES, AND ROLL OF HONOR

Tablets of the Missing, Cambridge, England (5,126 MIAs)

The Cambridge American Military Cemetery is the only WWII cemetery in the British Isles for Americans who died in WWII. The beautiful land was given to the United States by Cambridge University. It is a very impressive, moving, and beautiful memorial for the American soldiers, airmen, navy, marines, army, and coastguardsmen who died in WWII while stationed in the UK.

On the Tablets of the Missing (a high wall 427 feet long) are the names and particulars of 5,126 missing in action, lost or buried at sea, or those "unknowns" whose remains were either never found or positively identified prior to interment. The Cambridge grave area contains 3,812 American dead actually buried there. Most of these servicemen and servicewomen died in the Battle of the Atlantic or in the strategic air bombardment of Northwest Europe. Along the wall are four impressive statues carved by English craftsmen: a soldier, an airman, a sailor, and a coastguardsman.

The names of many men from the 95th BG are on the wall, including Lt. Fred A. Delbern and S/Sgt. Eugene F. Darter of the crew of the *Lonesome Polecat II* B-17F. As I enter the cemetery grounds and walk slowly down the path between the grave sites marked by white crosses just beyond the long lily pond on the left and the white stone engraved tablets of the missing on the right, I always walk to the airman statue and give it a hug because the statue now serves as a stand-in for my big brother. I then locate my brother's name and run my fingers slowly over the letters. This is always a deeply moving moment when I meet my brother each year. I only wish that our parents could have experienced this also.

Just beyond the end of the wall is the Cambridge memorial chapel. This is a most sacred place to honor those who fell. On the south exterior of the memorial is a great map, which depicts each location in the United Kingdom where an American unit or battalion or larger size was stationed during WWII. Inside the memorial, an impressive map, "The Mastery of the Atlantic—The Great Air Assault," is the outstanding feature of the museum room. The map shows miniature airplanes, ships, and other items related to the war in Europe. Fittingly, on the high ceiling of the Cambridge memorial are large images of B-17s, B-24s, and others on their way to their targets over the Third Reich, carrying many of the men who now rest in the cemetery and whose names are on the Tablets of the Missing.

I just returned from spending Memorial Day at the Cambridge American Cemetery in the UK. This was a most moving and beautiful ceremony with touching music, speeches, pipers, the Air Force Band, and the laying of many reefs for those killed and buried (3,811) and for those whose names are listed on the beautiful Wall of the Missing (5,126). Little has been written about the many MIAs, but in the 95th BG, I did a detailed count and found that about one out of every three killed in action are still missing. Yes, that is one-third whose families have little or no knowledge of how and where their son was killed, thus no closure. This proportion is more than the overall World War II MIA statistics of about one missing in every five KIA.

After the emotional and very impressive Memorial Day ceremony at Cambridge, I walked up to the long Wall of the Missing and ran my fingers over my brother's name and that of Fred Delbern (Don Neff is honored on the Wall of Missing at Margraten American Cemetery in Holland and is looked after by a caring Dutch family). Every year, I recommit myself to discovering what happened to these brave men who gave their lives for our freedom. The following is engraved in large letters along the stone wall at the Cambridge American Cemetery in the UK and explains this thought very well:

> *The Americans, whose names appear here, were part of the price that free men for the second time in this century have been forced to pay to defend human liberty and rights. All who shall hereafter live in freedom will be here reminded that to these men and their*

comrades we owe a debt to be paid with grateful remembrance of their sacrifice and high resolve that the cause for which they died shall live eternally.

Cambridge American Cemetery on Memorial Day, May 30
(Photo credit M. I. Darter)

Tablets of the Missing, Margraten, Holland

Lt. Don P. Neff of the crew of the *Polecat* B-17F is honored on similar Tablets of the Missing at the Netherlands American Military Cemetery and Memorial in Margraten, Holland, six miles east of Maastricht.

The Netherlands American Military Cemetery is beautiful and serene, with 8,301 graves and 1,723 names on the Tablets of the Missing. Photos of the Margraten cemetery are shown. The Dutch are so appreciative of the sacrifices of our fathers, brothers, and sons that each American grave was adopted by a Dutch family on the first Memorial Day after the war ended and that man's grave is passed down from generation to generation.

American military who are buried overseas or still missing in action are honored at these and other similar cemeteries. An extremely valuable database of WWII and other wars can be found on the American Battle Monuments Commission Web site (www.usabmc.com). There is a separate page of information on each of the three crew members (Darter, Delbern, and Neff).

The X-Files of American Unknowns

There exist twenty-four actual grave sites of unknown American military personnel at the Cambridge American Military Cemetery and 106 unknown gravesites at the Netherlands American Military Cemetery (Margraten). A photograph of one of these gravesites is shown below.

Grave site of an unknown American at the Cambridge
American Military Cemetery.

Unknown grave sites ("Known Only To God") are common at the twenty-four American military American cemeteries around the world. Each grave contains the remains of an Unknown that was unidentifiable. On the back of the headstone of each Unknown grave is an X-Number, specific to that cemetery that identifies the grave to a corresponding file of information that exists in the Department of Defense offices in Washington, D.C. I have heard that there are a few thousand of these X-files.

Of course, I have wondered for years if my brothers remains had washed ashore in the Wadden Sea or even North Sea (North Holland area) with no dog tag or other identifying marks, the remains would have been locally buried with some kind of marker and then disinterred by the American Graves Recovery teams that combed the area after the war. There would have been a forensic examination, and then if no identification was possible, the remains would have been sent for reburial at the Netherlands American Cemetery at Margraten. This is the cemetery that contains the Unknowns discovered in the North Netherlands area. It is clearly possible that S/Sgt. Eugene Francis Darter's remains exist as an Unknown with an X-Number in this cemetery. There are only 106 such Unknowns remaining at Margraten after many hundreds have been identified (and their families notified) thanks to thorough forensic investigation.

I have desired to examine the X-files for many years, but only recently realized that I could use the Freedom of Information Act to accomplish this task. I did just that at the Freedom of Information and Privacy Act Office, Army Human Resources Command's Freedom of Information Act program.(502) 613-4203. To my great delight several DVDs arrived just as this book was going to press that contain all of the Margraten X-flies. All documents in each X-file had been scanned and placed into one PDF file! I could now examine each Unknown file to see if there was any possibility that this could be my Eugene Darter. I was somewhat hopeful, but realizing the circumstances surrounding his being pulled out into the freezing Wadden Sea tethered to his parachute made it a very low probability that any of these Unknowns would be my brother.

As I began reviewing the X-files, I was indeed shocked at the details I encountered examining file after file of tragedy. However, I was impressed at the extreme care that those conducting this vital mission (both military and civilian staff) over decades had documented every aspect possible during the 40s and 50s of an Unknown so that they might be identified and returned home to their families for proper burial with honors.

One hundred and twenty seven X-files were included for those Unknowns who were buried at the American Margraten Cemetery. Since there are actually only 106 Unknowns buried at Margraten, there were several of these Unknowns that had been identified. The Unknowns buried in Margraten were initially found mainly in the Netherlands, Germany, and Belgium.

Some Unknowns were buried in local graveyards, some buried in isolated graves with wooden crosses hand marked as "American soldier" or "airman," some laying deceased near a glider crash, some in a severely burned US tank, a few pulled from the Rhine and other rivers, two in a German bombed hospital, some remains recovered from a bomber or fighter wreckage, and several washed up on the shore of the North Sea, Wadden Sea, or Ijsselmeer. The amount of the remains varied from nearly a full body to only a few pounds after complete decomposition.

In trying to identify any of these remains as my brother Eugene Darter, I searched first for anything that would eliminate the Unknown in the X-file information such as an early death date, inland location, or non-airman uniform. If no definite negatives were found, I then searched for any potential favorable identification characteristics such as physical description, tooth chart, and specific injury as Eugene was shot through the arm and leg. Three examples follow to show the depth of information for these Unknowns. Of course, for many Unknowns, there was much less information and their remains had been reduced to only a few pounds.

Designated Unknown X-2068 was found washed up on a beach near the Ijsselmeer village of Hindelopen on 18th of April 1944. A Dutch police officer went to the place and found the body (statement said "probably an American flyer") and brought it to the village. On 19th April 1944 a German investigated the body and found no identification other than he said it was an American nationality. The body was buried that day in the village cemetery at Plot D, Row 2, Grave 1, Hindelopen, Netherlands. The remains were disinterred 10 April 1947 to the American Margraten Cemetery, Netherlands (Plot PPP, Row 11, Grave 259).

Before reburial, a forensic investigation was conducted that included at least the following: statement that the remains were badly decomposed, clothing and equipment (none), member of Air, Ground, or Naval service (undeterminable), estimated age (undeterminable), height (6-ft), and weight (undeterminable), many characteristics about hair and facial hair (all undeterminable), skeletal chart that showed fingers missing, all flesh decomposed, original remains found in grave wrapped in burlap, no teeth.

Comment: The discovery of the remains four months after Eugene became MIA is favorable. However, Hindelopen, Netherlands is on the south side of the dike that separates the Wadden Sea from the Ijsselmeer and thus makes it unlikely that any remains could have crossed over. Also, the 6-ft height is much too tall for my brother.

Designated Unknown X-2004 was found washed up on the North Beach of the Netherlands Terschilling Island on 29th September 1944. The body was buried October 2, 1944 in the island Allied Cemetery and labeled: "126 One-Unknown U.S.A. Flyer". The remains were disinterred November 5, 1945 to the American Margraten Cemetery, Netherlands (Plot UU, Row 9, Grave 225).

Before reburial, a forensic investigation was conducted that included at least the following: statement that the remains were badly decomposed, clothing and equipment (trousers, undershirt, drawers size 32, shoes, wool socks, fleece boots size 7-D, electrically heated flying suite, flying coveralls), member of Army Air Force, estimated age (undeterminable), height (5-ft 4-in), weight (undeterminable), head circumference 21-in, many characteristics about hair and facial hair (all undeterminable), skeletal chart that showed fingers missing, tooth chart, trunk of body recovered intact with large amount of flesh in hard dry state.

Comment: Terschilling Island is 35 miles northeast of Texel. It is more likely Eugene's remains traveled south from Texel given the prevailing tide currents of the Wadden Sea. The discovery of the remains ten months after Eugene became MIA is not impossible if his Mae West was inflated and parachute became disconnected, both of which are unlikely. Favorable findings include clothing and equipment (trousers, undershirt, drawers size 32, shoes, wool socks, fleece boots size 7-D, electrically heated flying suite, flying coveralls), member of Army Air Force, height (5-ft 4-in), and head circumference 21-in. A tooth chart comparison was not clear and needs further professional investigation.

> Designated Unknown X-2015 was found washed ashore from the Wadden Sea near Oostmahorn, Netherlands. Statement: "Body picked up at Oostmahorn. Had stayed in water about 3 or 4 months. Picked up on 27 April 44 and buried April 29, 1944." Another statement: "Death of this unknown occurred somewhere over the sea. The body was washed ashore 27 April 1944. The body was taken to Anjum, Holland for burial." The body was buried in Row 16, Grave 13 in Anjum Cemetery. No marker was found on grave. Another statement: "Notebloc was taken by the Germans. Pocket comb and a fancy coloured handkerchief was found on the body, these were the only personal effects left on the body. A flying suit was marked on the collar: (unreadable)."
>
> The remains were disinterred November 9, 1945 to the American Margraten Cemetery, Netherlands (Plot VV, Row 11, Grave 255). Before reburial, a forensic investigation was conducted that included at least the following: statement that the remains were in last stage of decomposition, fleece lined flying boot, remnants of a leather jacket with Lt. bars sewn, summer flying suit, service shoes and English made size 8-E, wool socks, member of Army Air Force, estimated age (undeterminable), estimated height (5-ft 9-in), no teeth found, weight (undeterminable), head circumference (undeterminable), many characteristics about hair and facial hair (all undeterminable), skeletal chart that showed fingers missing. Statement: "Body was too decomposed and all identification gone because of period the body was in the water."

Comment: Anjum, Netherlands is on the mainland east side of the Wadden Sea about 60 miles northeast of Texel. It is possible that Eugene's remains could have eventually floated this far north in the Wadden Sea if his life vest was inflated and parachute disconnected. The discovery of the remains was four months after Eugene became MIA matches the statement that body was three or four months in the water. This also matches the statement that the body was decomposed because of the period in the sea. Both location and timing makes this Unknown a possibility. No tooth chart is available for comparison. Then main unfavorable aspect is the remnants of a leather jacket with a Lt. stripe on it. Darter was a Sergeant. The estimated height of 5-ft 9-in is taller than my brother at 5-ft 7-in.

Reviews of all of these X-files revealed a few interesting possibilities but with significant unfavorable characteristics. Reading one-hundred and twenty seven of these X-files has been a somber and saddening experience to more fully realize what these men went through to as they made the ultimate sacrifice. Our family is incredibly grateful to all of those military and other personnel who took such great care to document and identify as carefully as possible these Unknown remains of US military personnel. The still ongoing process to identify and bring home these Unknowns is an ever changing situation that will continue to yield more and more success, especially with modern day forensic technology.

Roll of Honor, St. Paul's Cathedral, London

During a visit with Doral Hupp (the crew member who helped my brother Eugene Darter out of the severely damaged B-17 after he was badly hit), he gave me a book titled *Britain's Homage to 28,000 American Dead* dated 1952, London, the Times, that had "In Memory of S/Sgt. E. F. Darter, USAAF." Doral and I read it to discover that after the war, the English government and people desired to honor the Americans based in England and Northern Ireland who had made the "ultimate sacrifice." The dean of St. Paul's, the Very Reverend Walter Matthews, suggested the cathedral as the location of a memorial chapel, and his idea was adopted. General Dwight D. Eisenhower was so moved by this offer that he offered all possible help. The British representatives declined and made it very clear that the chapel was to be a tribute from the people of their country to the Americans. President Eisenhower asked to be allowed to cooperate by preparing and presenting a Roll of Honor of those whose memory the chapel was intended to memorialize, which was accepted. A site for the chapel was chosen to be at the extreme east end of the beautiful cathedral that miraculously had avoided serious bomb damage while nearly everything around it was destroyed.

The Roll of Honor stands below the high altar and beneath its canopy. The central window of the chapel is the main stained-glass window of the cathedral. The chapel was dedicated in November 1958 in a ceremony attended by HM Queen Elizabeth II and Vice President Richard M. Nixon.

The Roll of Honor contains the names of over twenty-eight thousand Americans who gave their lives in aiding the United Kingdom and Northern Ireland during World War II. Each day, a different page of the book is opened on the altar. Most importantly, a copy of the book is available nearby on request for visitors to be shown names, which are listed alphabetically, followed by rank and service. My guide carefully turned the pages of the book for me to see the names of Lt. Frederick A. Delbern, Lt. Don P. Neff, and S/Sgt. Eugene F. Darter beautifully engraved in the book.

> *The beauty of the chapel lies in the love and dedication invested by everyday individuals. The chapel is love; and remains very breathtaking, solemn, heart wrenching and beautiful. It is a sanctuary of beauty paid for with a price we cannot ever repay.*[35]

Cambridge American Military Cemetery, England. Photo shows Tablets of the Missing with statues on the right, chapel in the center, and cemetery on the left. The names of S/Sgt. Eugene F. Darter and Lt. Fredrick Delbern are engraved on the wall along with over 5,000 other names. (Photo credit M. I. Darter)

Netherlands American Military Cemetery and Memorial in southern Holland in the village of Margraten, six miles east of Maastricht. The name of Lt. Don P. Neff is engraved on the Wall of the Missing. The nephew of S/Sgt. Eugene F. Darter, Paul J. Darter, is shown in the photo. (Photo credit M. I. Darter)

CHAPTER 22

MEMORIAL FOR CREW AND "MESSAGE FROM BEYOND"

Darter Family Arrives on Texel, May 3, 2007, for Memorial

In the summer of 2006, the Bürgermeister of Texel was contacted, and a date to hold a memorial for the three MIA crewmen who made the ultimate sacrifice was set for May 4, 2007. So a year later, the Darter family (five children and three grandchildren and spouses) arrived on Texel on an updated version of the *Dokter Wagemaker* ferry (that had helped saved the life of another American airman, Lt. Harold Kious, during the war) from Den Helder. When we went to the WWII museum, Bram Van Dijk and Johan Graas greeted us and excitedly handed us an obviously corroded and severely damaged piece of aluminum and steel that was found on the North Sea beach south from where the *Polecat* lies out in the water. They believed it was a piece of the *Polecat* wreckage.

This piece was subsequently identified as a "trim tab hinge" from a B-17F and was stamped manufactured by Alcoa Aluminum and included a ball bearing for the hinge labeled "Made in the USA." There are no other B-17 aircraft crashes within miles of this location. Can you imagine finding a piece of the aircraft sixty-four years after it crashed just off the Texel beach? Especially when this happened just days before a yearlong scheduled memorial for the crew who gave their lives? It was a very emotional and touching moment for our family.

Piece of the *Lonesome Polecat II* B17F found on the North Sea beach not far
from the wreckage that lies in about twenty feet of water one thousand feet
offshore, given to Michael Darter on May 3, 2007, by Bram Van Dijk
and Johan Graas at WWII Museum, Texel, Netherlands.
(Photo credit M. I. Darter)

The discovery of a piece of the *Polecat* on the beautiful Texel beach
just days before the memorial was published in newspaper headlines as,
"A Message from Beyond." And indeed, it certainly was interpreted that
way by the Darter family. We believe that these three young men, Fred,
Don, and Eugene, who paid the ultimate sacrifice, wanted us their family
and their former crewmates to know they were okay and for us to have
some closure.

Message from beyond

A piece of Staff Sgt. Eugene Darter's plane washes up on a beach in the Netherlands while his brother is there for a memorial service

Vanda Bidwell/The News-Gazette

Michael Darter of Champaign holds up a picture of his brother, Staff Sgt. Eugene Darter, and a piece of his brother's World War II plane. Staff Sgt. Darter died in 1943 in Texel, the Netherlands, when his plane crashed. A piece of the plane washed up on a beach recently.

By PAUL WOOD
pwood@news-gazette.com

Sixty-three years after a B-17 bomber crashed into the North Sea, a piece of the plane washed up on the beach.

It was a stunning moment for Michael Darter of Champaign, who was there for a memorial service for his brother, who had been on the plane and died in the frigid waters.

On May 3, Darter was in Holland, where a memorial was erected for his brother, the radio officer on the plane, missing in action since 1943.

"The Dutch told me my brother was sending me a message from the dead," said Darter, a University of Illinois emeritus professor of civil engineering. The piece of the plane that washed ashore had a part number that identified it.

Darter, 63, was just a baby when his 30-year-old brother Eugene came home on leave in 1943. His parents told him how the older brother flew him around the room on a pillow, but he is too young to remember it.

Please see BROTHERS, A-6

The crew of Staff Sgt. Darter's doomed flight during 1943. It was the crew's first bombing raid.

News Gazette Newspaper (Champaign, Illinois) front page for 7 May 2007 describing the "Message From Beyond" found on Texel beach the week before the memorial. The Darter family and local Texel residents were shocked by the discovery sixty-four years after the nearby crash of the aircraft. (Image credit News Gazette Newspaper)

Darter family at the May 4, 2007, memorial held for the three MIA airmen of the *Lonesome Polecat II* at the WWII Monument, Texel, Netherlands (Photo credit M. I. Darter)

Presentation of the memorial wreath and a plaque on the Lancaster World War II Monument by the Bürgermeister Joke Geldorp of Texel, NL for the three MIA airmen (Photo credit M. I. Darter)

Ceremony at the Texel Lancaster Dike World War II Memorial, May 7, 2007

Over one hundred Texel residents came to the memorial the next day. The Bürgermeister of Texel gave a beautiful memorial of respect and honor from the Dutch people for the sacrifice of the *Lonesome Polecat II* crew. She laid a beautiful wreath at the World War II memorial. We then unveiled a small plaque for S/Sgt. Eugene F. Darter, showing him coming down in a parachute which temporarily saved his life. Johan Graas introduced the entire crew by name and position and gave a summary of their mission and fate.

The following section of a 1945 letter from crew member Charlie Schreiner to pilot Fred Delbern's wife was read by Michael Darter as a tribute to Lt. Fred A Delbern, plane commander:

> *Our entire crew was strongly attached to Freddie. Each man in the crew admired, respected and loved Fred in a man's way . . . Del always treated every man in the crew equally and with consideration. As a plane commander he could not be beat and as a pilot he was aces. Us guys should know because we lived and breathed flying together. Del often said to other pilots that he felt plenty lucky that he had a crew of competent men.*
>
> *When the showdown came, we gave our best. Personally, I feel confident every man in our crew was qualified to carry his job through to the end without question or hesitation. Our ten men fought splendidly as a team and I am proud that I had the privilege to fight side by side with such swell guys. Under desperate combat conditions you find exactly what men are made of—and that is why I feel as strongly as I do about my crewmates.*

Michael Darter, brother of Eugene Darter, gave a special memorial to his brother. He also showed the "Message from Beyond" trim tab hinge from the *Polecat* B-17F that was discovered on the beach the week prior. We were all somewhat speechless.

Several of the attendees were actual eyewitnesses, who more than sixty years ago, had seen the badly damaged and stricken B-17 (*Lonesome Polecat II*) roar just over their village of De Koog, climb over the high row of dunes, and finally crash just off the Texel beach in the North Sea. This included Michelle Binsbergen and Cees Bonnie who saw and heard the *Polecat* roar over their heads in the village of De Koog. Other eyewitnesses had also seen some of the crew land either on the island or, in S/Sgt. Darter's case, in the Wadden Sea. This included P. K. Stark who met wounded Sgt. Charles Schreiner and Bob McKeegan coming out of the dunes under guard by Nazi soldiers.

More on the Trim Tab Hinge

There are actually four trim tab hinges on a B-17F: one on the rudder, one on each horizontal stabilizer, and one on a wing. Further examination of the trim tab hinge piece revealed a ball bearing that was inscribed as shown below.

Trim tab hinge including the ball bearing from a B17 (there are four of these on a B17). This severely damaged piece was found on North Sea beach south of the *Polecat* crash site in April 2007 just before the memorial.
(Photo credit M. I. Darter)

Close-up of trim tab ball bearing hinge from B17 discovered on Texel
North Sea beach. Note the inscription "Made in USA." Note also
the inscription "Fafnir." (Photo credit M. I. Darter)

An Internet search of Fafnir revealed amazingly that this ball bearing
was manufactured in the USA by the Fafnir Ball Bearings Co., the leading
maker of ball bearings as shown in their 1942 advertisement, "Fafnir
Bearing Co., 23 tons of prodigious flying might" (*Aviation*, July, 1942, p.
16). Note that a B-17 photo is included in the advertisement.

Fafnir ball bearings for aircraft engines and controls[53]

Certainly, this discovery coming sixty-four years after the crash and the timing of this discovery just days before the memorial to the three MIA crew was quite shocking and left our family believing that indeed miracles still happen. It also helped to confirm that this piece of wreckage was from a B17 and that there are no other B17 crashes within miles of De Koog village.

The next year, I finally met the man who found the piece on the beach. His name is Paul Dekker of Texel, who had been out regularly with a metal detector on the beach and had found several other pieces along with several .50-caliber machine gun cartridges dated 1943 DM (for the Des Moines, Iowa, ammunition plant). Other cartridges were dated 1943 SL (for the Salt Lake City, Utah, ammunition plant). These damaged pieces tend to show the plane hit quite hard into the water, and that is likely why pilot Fred Delbern, very sadly, did not survive the crash.

Paul Dekker found pieces of the *Lonesome Polecat II* on the Texel North Sea beach before the May 4, 2007, memorial and more afterward. Note that the "foreign pieces" lying on the normally pristine white sand beach showed up in early 2007. (Photo credit M. I. Darter)

Discovery of Additional Pieces of B-17F Polecat and Ammunition on the Beach in 2008 through 2013

Annual visits were made to Texel between 2008 and 2013. I first met Paul Dekker of Texel in 2008, who had found the "trim tab hinge" from the

B-17F and took the piece to the museum just before the *Polecat* memorial on May 4, 2007. Paul has very kindly given our family the pieces of the aircraft and all the .50-caliber machine gun shell casings dated 1943 that he found on the beach with his metal detector between 2007 and 2013. Eight of these casings were marked DM 43 and one SL 43. Research shows that the DM casings were manufactured in the Des Moines, Iowa, USA, ammunition plant and the SL casing in the Salt Lake City, Utah, USA, ammunition plant in 1943. These shells were shot by the *Polecat* crew from positions at attacking enemy fighters and fell on the floor of the aircraft and then washed out during and after the crash. Another piece thought to be part of the top turret and small piece of Plexiglas from the aircraft were also discovered.

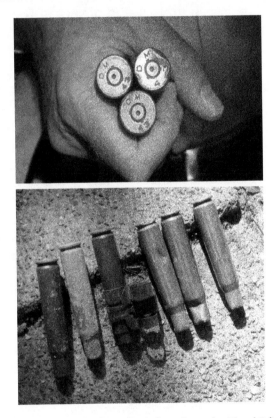

The .5-caliber machine gun brass casings found on the Texel Island beach from 2007 to 2013 by Paul Dekker. All were dated 1943 and shot at enemy fighters attacking the *Polecat*, initially falling on the aircraft floor, and then washed out during and after the crash near Paal #19. Damage to some shell casings indicates the *Polecat* hit the water hard. (Photo credit M. I. Darter)

How these small pieces of the *Polecat* and spent shell casings suddenly showed up south of the sunken and covered-with-sand aircraft wreckage site on the North Sea beach sixty-four years after the crash is a mystery. Lots of discussions with many local people were held over this very unlikely event. The most plausible explanation of this mystery evolves from government efforts to control the severe erosion from big waves and storms from the North Sea.

There is lots of beach erosion from major storms that come in from the North Sea throughout the year. For many years, the government has been dredging up sand far out in the North Sea in large boats and then depositing the sand several hundred feet out in the water along the Texel beach, including beach marker Paal #19. I have observed this activity several times during the past thirteen years of visits to Texel.

This sand covered the *Polecat* wreckage field for decades after the 1981 and 1984 fishing boats loss of their nets near Paal 19 on the sunken wreckage. Then in 2007, a portion of the beach between Paal 15 and Paal 18 eroded badly. To replace the missing sand, a dredging operation near the *Polecat* wreckage field sucked up some of the sand and blew it out on the beach between Paal #15 and #18.

There suddenly appeared on the beach lots of foreign materials and rocks in this area between Paal #15 and #18 in 2007. Some of this material was from the aircraft wreckage field, consisting of loose pieces and especially spent brass casings of .5-caliber machine gun shells. Note that the *Polecat* was filled with seven thousand shell casings from the crew shooting at enemy attackers, so these were sucked up along with other pieces from the crash site. These were then blown out onto #15 to #18 beach area.

In this area, Paul Dekker found several metal and Plexiglas pieces, and some of these were clearly B-17F parts, including the trim tab hinge and nine shell casings dated 1943 from the *Polecat* as shown below. No doubt there have been many more picked up by beachcombers and tourists since 2007. There is no doubt that in the future, additional pieces of the *Polecat* will be recovered in the General area and shed more understanding on these quite amazing discoveries. These are all more pieces of the grand puzzle of this mystery that have been discovered.

This Google Maps imagery shows the General area around Paal #19 where just off the Texel beach the *Polecat* crashed. Note the local disturbance of the sand just to the bottom of the sunken B-17F image where it is believed a dredging operation took place in 2007, sucking up pieces of the wreckage field and then depositing the sand and wreckage pieces south along the beach between Paal #15 and #18 where the wreckage pieces were discovered. Another miracle! (Image credit Google Imagery)

CHAPTER 23

DISCOVERY OF WIVES OF LT. FRED DELBERN AND LT. DON NEFF

The surviving crew told me that both pilots were married and that they had met the wife of Lt. Fred Delbern as she had traveled with him during their time in Spokane and was there the day the crew departed for England. Ms. Delbern had visited with Doral Hupp after the war, trying desperately to find out what happened to her missing husband. Personally, I had no hope at all in ever finding either woman after so many years. Both would likely have remarried after all hope of their husbands returning had been lost and thus would have different names and possibly moved to different cities. But then again, it seems like almost anything is possible with this search for the missing.

Discovery of Wife of Pilot Lt. Fred Delbert, March 2009

We actually did not find her. Beyond all belief, the former wife of pilot Lt. Fred Delbern found us in March 2009. We received a call from the nephew of the former Mrs. Delbern Dane Hanson, informing us that she was indeed still alive, had discovered the book *Fateful Flight of the Lonesome Polecat*[46] published in 2004 (Fred's photo on cover), and very much wanted to talk to us. Wow, everyone associated with the *Polecat* were surprised and amazed. I called her immediately, and she had indeed remarried after she visited Doral after the war and all hope of Fred returning was lost. The former Mrs. Delbern, now Geraldine Marshall, had a good, long sixty-one-year second marriage to Joe Marshall before he died in 2008. Her family knew that her first husband was a veteran lost in the war and suggested she apply for veterans benefits. She already knew practically from memory the necessary information such as the name of the aircraft, *Lonesome Polecat II*, and its serial number (#42-30255). These were given to Geri by crewmate Charlie Schreiner in an eight-page typed letter dated November 1945,[36] as well as letters from the War Department after Fred became missing.

Geri's nephew Charlie Hanson Goggled the *Lonesome Polecat* and immediately up popped the cover of the book *Fateful Flight of the Lonesome Polecat II* written by the author in 2004[46] that had Fred's crew photo on the cover. She was so shocked she could hardly speak and cried for joy to possibly now discover what happened to Fred, the love of her life. Geri immediately ordered the book and read it and read it and read it and discovered the details she has longed to know about her beloved first husband's fateful mission over Bremen, Germany.

After talking to Geri by telephone, I traveled to Duluth, Minnesota, and met her and shared all the photographs of Texel and the details of what we knew about the crew and Fred's mission. I also met her family members Dane Hanson and Charlie Hanson.

Geraldine Delbern Marshall (former wife of Lt. Fred Delbern), Charles Hanson (left), and Dane Hanson (right) (Photo credit M. I. Darter)

Last photo of Geri and Fred the day he and his crew departed for England in October 1943. Geri told me, "This is what happiness looks like!"
(Photo credit Geri Delbern Marshall)

During my meetings with Geri, who is soon to be ninety-five years young and living in Duluth, Minnesota, she says that her forever-handsome young lieutenant is in her first thoughts every day as she awakens and looks at his photo on her dresser.

They were married on May 2, 1942, and spent a wonderful few months together before he joined up for the US Army Air Corps. Geri talks about Fred as a very happy and outgoing young man who was a top-notch athlete in basketball, football, and track and field, with his name and photos often in the Duluth newspapers in high school. However, football was his main love, and Fred was very good at it as shown by his football scholarship to the University of Minnesota.

Fred was also a very good singer and had sung for many occasions in Duluth. In fact, at Christmas mass in December 1942, he surprised her with a solo of "O Holy Night," which of course thrilled Geri.

The other thing that Fred loved was flying. He learned to fly a single-seat aircraft and had received his pilot's license before he enlisted in the Army Air Corps. Geri relates, "I wanted him to wait and be drafted like everybody else. But he was crazy about flying, and he enlisted. When I found out, I didn't like it very well."[41] Fred was sent to several bases in Alabama, Georgia, and Florida and finally ended up in Spokane, Washington, when his crew was formed.

Geri stayed in a Spokane hotel with other wives while Fred and his crew trained intensively and endlessly, getting ready for that day they would be assigned overseas and sent into combat against the most technologically advanced air force in the world. Geri said that a few times, Fred's crew came over to the hotel and played poker, and then they'd go down and have a drink. "Everyone on the crew was so nice, and they were all so young. Of course, I was very young too."[41]

She met all of the crew members, including my brother Eugene, and she told me that he was a very kind, happy, and dedicated man. Geri last saw Fred in the hotel in Spokane. Fred took Geri to a store and bought her a new dress, and then they had the above photo taken the same day. Geri kissed Fred good-bye with a heavy heart, and he told her, "*Auf wiedersehen* (good-bye, till we meet again)" and watched him turn and walked slowly down the hotel stairs, never imagining that was the last time she would see the love of her life. He and his crew then flew off to Nebraska to be outfitted with all of their flying gear before departing for war in Europe in early November 1943.

Geri returned home to Duluth and began writing to Fred every day, telling him of her love and his family's love for him. Thanksgiving and then Christmas December 1943 came and went with no word at all from Fred. Her anxiety and worry about Fred increased greatly. Then on New Year's Eve 1943, Geri lay down on the sofa and put a record on the phonograph and lay back. Suddenly, "I saw Fred. He was right next to me. He put his arm over mine, and touched my right arm. He had a big smile on his face. It was so real. I was sure I was not sleeping."[41] A little while later, there was a knock on the door, and it was a Western Union telegram stating that Fred was missing in action on December 16. Of course, this message broke her heart, and she went into a time of great sadness. Geri called Fred's family and told his mother, who idolized her only son. Geri's priest told her that only saints come back, but Geri knows the reality of what happened.

She was in agony for the next year and a half when the war finally ended in Europe in May 1945 and all the POWs were returned home. But Fred did not come home, and there was no additional information about him (other than the same as previous) even though she had written numerous letters asking for more information. She and her mother visited crew member Doral Hupp in Ohio, seeking information, and Doral tried to console her, telling Geri everything he knew about what happened to Fred. He and Charlie were the last to see Fred as he came out of the cockpit and talked to Doral. She then wrote to Charlie Schreiner in Burbank, California, pleading with him to tell her everything he knew about what happened to Fred. Charlie sat down and typed out a very detailed eight-page letter to Geri describing in detail what occurred on the mission to Bremen, Germany, on December 16, 1943. At the end, Charlie described that as he came down in his parachute, he watched overhead the severely damaged B-17 flying toward England, leaving a trail of smoke, with Fred and copilot Don Neff in the cockpit, and he wondered himself what the pilots would do.

In fact, it was not until February of 2009 when she discovered the book *Fateful Flight of the Lonesome Polecat II* did she learn the details of what happened to the love of her life over Texel Island so long ago. She read how Fred bravely had remarkably piloted the severely damaged B-17F from Bremen to Texel Island after being hit in his arm and his face blackened from smoke and the tragic death of his copilot sitting just next to him in the cockpit. As Geri told author Rob Morris recently, "Each morning, as Geri goes about her daily routine in her apartment in Duluth, she sees the smiling, handsome face of her husband Fred Delbern, and she feels a mixture of great sadness and peace. For he isn't really gone. He's inside her heart, and has been there for seventy years."[41]

Discovery of Wife of Copilot Lt. Don Neff, April, 2009

Lt. Don Neff was twenty-six years old and born in Bryan, Ohio. After searching for years, we have recently found the family genealogy records as well as Don's grandnephew Garry Neff in Ohio. A memorial was held at Pioneer, Ohio, one year after Don was reported missing. Don's mother, the former Elizabeth Poulson, reported that he had been assumed dead by the Army Air Corps one year after becoming missing. An obituary of his wife, Marjorie Staley Neff, was located, which stated she had passed away in 1984 in Spokane, Washington. She had remarried after the war and had two sons, one of whom was Brian Burk from her second husband. Brian graciously sent a photo of his mother Marjorie and Lt. Neff just after they were married in Spokane, Washington, just a few days before the crew departed for England. Marjorie too was heartbroken and devastated at the loss of her husband, feeling that immense pain of not knowing what had happened to Don.

Lt. Donald Neff, copilot, and Marjorie Staley were married on October 7, 1943, in Spokane, Washington. Don also kissed his new bride good-bye in Spokane, joined his crew, and departed for England, and the war occurred shortly thereafter, and he never returned. The tragedy of war lingers on for Generations. (Photo credit United States Army Air Corps)

There are many stories just like this one where two young people like Don and Marjorie and Fred and Geri meet and fall madly in love and marry just before he must depart for war, and then he vanishes and never returns home. She is devastated by his loss, and in many cases, nothing is known about what happened to him, so closure in her life does not happen. The B-17 that Don Neff was copiloting just "disappeared into clouds west of Bremen, Germany," was all the letters from the government stated.

One consolation is that a Dutch family has "adopted" Don's "grave" site in 2013, which for an MIA is his name engraved on the Tablets of the Missing at Margraten American Cemetery in the Netherlands. This is a beautiful and sacred cemetery with a large gray stone wall containing the Tablets of the Missing, with the names of many young men engraved on it. The Dutch family has been provided with all the information and photos we have on Don and have visited the Tablets of the Missing and placed flowers there probably for only the second time since the monument was established decades ago (the author and his son Paul visited Margraten and found Don's name and honored him in 2002).

Don Neff and crewmate Pete Jackson were best of friends. Pete told me that they did a lot of things together and that he really admired Don Neff. When Pete (the navigator) heard the bailout alarm, he crawled up to the cockpit and saw Don in his seat helping fly the stricken bomber. He said to him, "Come on, Don, let's get out of here." But pilot Delbern of course needed Don to help fly the badly damaged aircraft until the rest of the crew got out and could not let him go at that time.

Moments later, Don was hit by shrapnel from 20-mm shells from an attacking German fighter and was fatally wounded in his copilot's seat. This happened in just the moment between Pete, Ed, and Loren bailing out (they reported Don as not injured) and the US fighter escort arriving that drove off the German fighters and saved the remainder of the crew on board the *Polecat*. Just minutes before reaching Texel, Doral asked Fred about Don, and Fred told Doral to "forget about Don." Doral took this to mean that Don had sadly been fatally wounded in the copilot's seat.

Based on all of the information available about the final minutes of the flight and the German interrogator telling Charlie Schreiner that two bodies were found in the sunken aircraft, we believe that Don's remains are also in the cockpit of the *Polecat* just off the shore at beach marker #19 near De Koog, Texel.

CHAPTER 24

GONE WITH THE WIND

G iven the knowledge that my brother Eugene was the first to bail out and the locations of his crewmates as they landed across the island, it is obvious that he splashed down in the icy waters of the Wadden Sea somewhere between the European coast and the Texel dike near the village of Oost. It was hard to imagine that anyone could have seen his parachute come through the thick fog and cloud cover or heard his last cries for help. Well, read on and experience with me this last unbelievable discovery in the mystery of what happened to MIA S/Sgt. Eugene F. Darter.

My Most Incredible Discovery

The distance across the Wadden Sea from the main Dutch coast and Texel Island is about twenty-one miles along the flight path from Bremen. It is certain that Eugene bailed out a few minutes before Bob, Doral, Frank, and Charlie, who all landed on and across the five-mile-wide island. Doral's estimate of the time between Eugene's departure and Bob's was four minutes. Given the speed of the *Polecat* means he could have landed a few miles from the island, too far out for anyone to see or hear him on a very foggy, stormy, and freezing day in December. Never in my wildest dreams did I think that we could discover what happened to my brother after he hit the freezing seawater, let alone what happened to his remains over sixty years ago. This is indeed a very cold case.

I was quite hopeful, however, that we could find eyewitnesses of the low-flying B-17F roaring over the island and also of the bailout and capture of four crew by the Nazis even considering sixty years had passed. People don't forget these kinds of traumatic events that occurred even in their younger lives. The Texel newspaper, the *Texelse Courier*, and reporter Mr. Timmerman were very supportive of our search and published every year an article I wrote, asking for help in finding eyewitnesses.

During one visit, my son Paul and I were again on Texel searching for information and helped Mr. Timmerman of the *Texelse Courier* newspaper prepare another article on the story and made another plea for anyone with information to come forward. Within a few days after returning home, two letters were received from residents of Texel that contained eyewitness accounts that provided some incredible information. Chapters 13 and 14 describe the information received from Mr. Cees Bonnie and his brother Nick and Mr. Michele Binsbergen that were children standing in their village of De Koog, hearing the roar and then experiencing the terrifying sight and sounds of a low-flying B-17 just over their homes, the Germans shooting at it with their rifles and then the plane barely clearing the high dunes and finally crash-landing in the North Sea just off the beach. It was really remarkable, to say the least, to know that Lt. Delbern had made the decision to ditch the *Polecat* near the Texel beach rather than to fly on over the North Sea where the *Polecat* would likely have exploded and disappeared into the North Sea as many B-17s and B-24s did.

Then just a couple of days after the above information were received, an e-mail came in one morning from a Mr. Cornelius J. Ellen, a lifelong resident of Texel. Cornelius had read the latest newspaper article we wrote, asking for information about an event that occurred sixty years ago, and he recalled immediately that on a very cold December day when he was seventeen, he saw an airman splash down in the Wadden Sea just off the Texel dike near his home. The event had traumatized him and had always made him feel depressed over the ensuing years that he could not help the airman and had to watch him die out in the sea. Here are his words in the e-mail sent by his sister Jenny from Texel[27] to me.

- Texel, 03-09-2002

- Dear Sir,

- About the lost member of the crew B17 on 16-12-1943,
- local newspaper De Texelse Courant

- On this day I (then age 17) am witness with eyes and ears when the air-man with his chute past the dike on a level of hight ± 150 m. Before he hit the sea water I hear his (a shrill) clear voice: 'Help me, Help me'. He came down ± 300 meter out of the dike in the sea (high tide), standing in the sea water till his breast/neck. The chute at that moment is laying down on the water, but this poor air-man did do nothing to get the chute down (wind force 4/5 bft, west direction).
- I ran away to get a kind of rescue boat, near the place. Half on the way for a rescue boat I looked behind me, and saw the wind is blowing into the chute and like a half-moon in the Wadden sea water take this poor air-man with it.

- 'Gone with the wind' between the farmhouses 'Sint Williebrord' and 'De Bemes'.

- I am, after nearly 60 years satisfied to send you this.
- Yours sincerely,

- Cornelis J. Ellen
- Osterstraat 3
- 1794 AR Oosterend - Texel / Holland
- Tel. +31 222 318 601

E-mail received from Cornelius Ellen of Texel Island, Netherlands, describing the American airman he saw when he was a young man (Image credit M. I. Darter)

"Gone with the wind!" When I read this, I could not control my emotions and closed my office door, and tears flowed down my face. I read it again and again. Gone with the wind! Could this be my brother Eugene that the seventeen-year-old Cornelius Ellen saw splash down into the Wadden Sea so close to the shore sixty years ago? The three hundred meters is about one thousand feet out where he splashed down and was not able to get into the shore for help. It appeared that the airman could not unbuckle himself from the parachute that he was then pulled by the wind further out into the Wadden Sea where he vanished from view from the shore. "Gone with the wind," was Cornelius's description. Unbelievably sad!

I immediately called Mr. Ellen on Texel and had a long emotional discussion with him concerning what he saw (thankfully for me, he spoke good English). Everything appeared to match what we knew already (e.g., the airman's condition, the weather, the afternoon timing, and the flight path). When I told Cornelius that Eugene was shot through the arm, he understood why he could not unbuckle the parachute, which had been a mystery to him for decades since this was the first thing an airman should have done.

I then called my dear friend Johan Graas who lives between Amsterdam and Texel to visit Mr. Ellen and talk in more detail, which he soon did, and he became convinced that Cornelius Ellen had seen the last moments of my brother's life. This information was overwhelming to me and my five children and of course the four surviving crew members Doral, Loren, Charlie, and Pete and all the families involved. Over time and many conversations later with Cornelius, it became obvious that he had truly seen my brother come down through the clouds and fog just over his head, screaming for help, but splashed down way too far out in the freezing Wadden Sea for Cornelius to help him on that cold winter's day without dying himself from hypothermia.

My brother came so close to surviving, but as Cornelius and I discussed over and over again on subsequent visits, several events went against Eugene, and "if only one" were different, he would likely have survived.

- If Eugene had waited just a few more seconds to bail out with the rest of the crew as Doral told him, he would have landed on the island with the other men and not one thousand feet (three hundred meters) offshore. However, neither he nor the crew had any idea there was an island down there through the thick undercast, and Eugene undoubtedly believed he had to get out of the dangerously burning aircraft and get to a hospital to save his life as he had lost so much blood. In reality, Doral, Charlie, Frank, and Bob were incredibly fortunate to have landed on the island twenty-one miles out from the main Dutch coastline, as they bailed out believing they would land in the North Sea and perish in the freezing waters, as was the fate of so many airmen escaping from badly war-damaged aircraft.

- If there had not been a stiff wind blowing out into the sea, Eugene would have landed securely on the island. He actually bailed out over the island but was blown offshore farther out into the Wadden Sea.

- If the tide was lower, Cornelius would have walked out and carried Eugene to the shore (the tide was beginning to go out when he splashed down as described in chapter 13). The difference in sea level from high to low tide is about 1.5 meters or five feet. Over the past several years, Cor and I and my family have walked out into the Wadden Sea for over one thousand feet when the tide is out and were in only a couple inches of water.

- And of course if he could have unbuckled his chute (e.g., as with a modern parachute), he would not have been pulled by the parachute shrouds out farther into the freezing Wadden Sea by the fierce wind where he quickly experienced hypothermia (loss of body temperature). He likely could have walked into shore with help from Cornelius and his friend, who would have gone right out and brought him to the shore and medical treatment.

Eugene actually experienced very cold temperatures after he was hit in the arm and leg, shooting out the top radio room hatch, and collapsed on the subzero aircraft floor, bleeding profusely from his arm for about twenty-five minutes, and then, with Doral's help, bailed out at about five thousand feet, landing in the freezing Wadden Sea where body heat was lost even more quickly as cold water filled his flying suit. As he was pulled out farther into the Wadden Sea by wind in the silk parachute, he blacked out and drowned in a minute or two, similar to American airman Harold Kious described in chapter 12.

When I called Loren, Charlie, and Doral and told them what I had just discovered, they too became very emotional as they had speculated for decades what had happened to Eugene. They particularly found it difficult to learn that Eugene had landed so close to the Texel shore and did not survive while they had so fortunately come down on the island, which saved their lives. Especially Doral felt sad because he had literally saved Eugene's life by stopping his bleeding and buckling his parachute on so he could open it with his only good arm. Doral told Eugene to wait until he had his parachute on and was ready to jump together. Had Eugene waited, he would have landed near Doral securely in the middle of Texel Island and most likely received medical treatment and survived.

Eugene's Last Moments

Imagine what Eugene Darter experienced as he looked out the rear side door and saw nothing but dense undercast below and began wondering what was down there. Probably the freezing North Sea since they had been flying for a long time. He was very weak from the loss of blood and the numbing cold, and he had to get medical attention. Nevertheless, he bravely jumped out of the door, dropped beneath the aircraft, and pulled his chute chord with his left hand as Doral had prepared him to do. The chute blossomed as seen by his crewmates as he soon entered into the clouds and fog. Suddenly, everything was white and deathly quiet compared to the roar of the engines and vibration of the aircraft.

As he emerged from the clouds and fog, he realized that he was being blown very rapidly eastward by a high wind. Eugene immediately saw farms and houses below, and his heart leaped as he thought, "Oh my god, there is land below, not the freezing North Sea and certain death." He also glanced at a large stately windmill off to his right but suddenly realized he was being blown rapidly eastward toward the sea just ahead. He sailed fast and uncontrollably (these chutes were circular and not controllable) directly over the heads of two boys walking along a large dike. All too quickly, he splashed down into the cold sea still buckled to his chest parachute, which landed in the water next to him.

As Eugene flew uncontrollably just one hundred meters (three hundred feet) over the boys' heads (Cornelius and his friend Bram), he called out to them in a shrill desperate voice, "Help me, help me," before splashing down in the sea. He tried but could not even begin to unbuckle the stiff metal snaps that attached his chest parachute to his harness with one arm and the freezing temperatures and weakness from loss of blood. The freezing water quickly filled his flying suit and underclothing as waves splashed over him as he stood on the bottom of the seabed with water up to his neck. He could still see the boys on the very high large dike but saw one of them running, perhaps for help. He tried and tried to unbuckle the stiff metal snaps that attached his chest parachute, but even his good hand was numb and very weak. He started shaking uncontrollably in the cold water.

Seconds later, the fierce wind unbelievably pulled his silk parachute partially out of the water and blew it into a half moon (as Cornelius observed from the dike), and the chords tightened and began pulling him farther out into the sea. He resisted the pull of the parachute shrouds, but in his weakened state, he was totally helpless to bring the half-moon parachute back into the water. As he was dragged along, he realized he was on a one-way ride farther out into the freezing sea. Just like Harold Kious who landed just to the south also in freezing temperatures, Eugene's vision blackened, and he began losing consciousness. He fought it off, but it came again and again as his body temperature dropped, and soon hypothermia took over, and he paid the ultimate sacrifice for his country.

His last thoughts were likely of his loving mother Estella and father Frank, his sister Hazel, and yes, maybe even his baby brother whom he carried around on that pillow, who would someday come searching for him.

Cornelius (or Cor) Ellen's Observations

Seventeen-year-old Cor knew that the airman was an American because the English bombers did not fly in the daytime. Both Cor and his friend Bram were shocked at what they saw, and Cor still feels very badly today that he could not help the airman because the parachute had pulled him out way too far and he would have died in the attempt. But seeing the airman die in front of him has haunted him for the many decades. It is obvious that without a boat immediately available, there was nothing he could do, as he would have quickly drowned trying to reach the airman so far out with the waves from a strong wind. Boats were prohibited on the dike by the Nazis, so he could have been shot if caught. The weather was very cold and the wind very strong (15-25 mph) out to sea. Cornelius lived nearby and returned to the place many times during subsequent days but never saw any remains washed ashore.

The location where this occurred matches well with the expected flight path where the *Polecat* crossed the eastern side of Texel near the village of Oost. Mr. Ellen saw this airman just north of the village of Oost, along the straight long dike just north of the old stately working windmill. There exists today an old concrete marker along the dike fence inscribed 18.3 that marks the exact location. After Mr. Ellen read the *Texelse Courier* newspaper account that we wrote, he could not sleep for a couple of nights, thinking about this, and then wrote his e-mail to me, which has brought some closure to our family and to his surviving crewmates, as well as himself.

A Surprising Coincidence or Help from Beyond?

We all have had the experience of receiving vital information and either ignoring it or forgetting about it. Well, thank God Cornelius Ellen read the newspaper article and contacted me by e-mail thereby giving our family a gift beyond measure.

I too had received some critical information and promptly forgot about it a week before when my son Paul and I were on Texel. During the visit to Texel, we had dinner one night at a nice restaurant in the village of De Koog (where the B-17F flew over). A waitress whose name was Naomi served us because she was fluent in English. We all had a wonderful time talking to her through the evening, and at one point, she asked us what we Americans were doing on Texel since this is not a typical American vacation spot. We told her we were searching for information about my brother who was shot down near Texel during the war. She said to us, "Then you should talk to my father-in-law because he lived during the war and knows a lot about what happened." We thanked her, and she wrote his name on a piece of paper for us, and I put it into my briefcase. One day, several months later, I found the note and read the name on it: Cornelius Ellen!

An Emotional Visit to Texel by Crewmate Doral Hupp

One extraordinary visit to Texel was with crewmate Doral Hupp and his lovely wife Winnie and family including son Rod. Recall that Doral had temporarily saved the life of my brother on the B-17F by stopping his bleeding and snapping his chute on upside down so that he could pull the pin with his left hand. Otherwise, Eugene could not have opened his chute. Doral was very anxious to see what the island looked like that he had luckily landed on nearly sixty years ago and where three of his crewmates died. He joked that "it was especially good to be back with no guns pointing at him." He was warmly welcomed by Texel residents. A luncheon was held at Hotel Opduin in De Koog near the crash site of the B17F, with the remains of pilots Fred Delbern and Don Neff. All of the participants enjoyed lunch and told their stories. A photo of the participants is below.

Back, left to right: Gerrit Betsema, Bram Van Dijk, Michele Binsbergen (eyewitness of the B-17F), Cornelius Ellen (eyewitness of Eugene Darter). Front, left to right: Michael Darter, Doral Hupp (original crew member), Johan Graas, Jack Betsema (father who saw the B-17F), Insert Cees Bonnie (eyewitness of the B-17F) (Photo credit M. I. Darter)

Given all of the evidence available, I have concluded that seventeen-year-old Cornelius Ellen saw my brother, S/Sgt. Eugene Darter, badly wounded and weakened from much loss of blood come down through the heavy overcast, crying for help, just barely missing the Texel shore, and splashing down at high tide in the Wadden Sea. What an incredible sequence of bad luck! Mr. Ellen has since very thoughtfully placed a pole and a concrete block as a marker out in the Wadden Sea where S/Sgt. Darter landed, which can be seen from the dike (marker 18.3).

I first saw the site, along with crew member Doral Hupp (who helped Eugene in the plane), when we traveled to Texel together. It was a deeply moving experience for both of us. My brother came so close to surviving. Bailing out just a couple of seconds later would have landed him securely on the island. Or if the water level was not at high tide, he could have walked into shore from where he landed, as the Wadden Sea is very shallow as observed on many subsequent visits. The bottom of the Wadden Sea can be seen for over a half mile out from the shore at low tide. It was actually shocking to see how shallow the Wadden Sea is at this location during low tide. If only this was the situation on that fateful day.

Seventeen-year-old Cornelius Ellen was walking with a friend along this dike in the afternoon of December 16, 1943, when suddenly, a parachute carrying an airman appeared out of the mist above him, flying directly over his head and out into the Wadden Sea. Note the old windmill at the top of the photo, which is just north of the village of Oost, Texel, Netherlands. The airman came down across the top of the dike from right to left in the photo. (Photo credit M. I. Darter)

There I stood on the dike sixty years after the event with Doral Hupp and Cornelius Ellen, the two people who last saw my brother alive, Doral in the plane and Cornelius in the seawater. This moment will be etched in my mind forever. We were together at last. It finally brought closure for me and Doral and Cornelius and the other surviving crew members after so many years of uncertainty.

Since then, Cornelius and I and my children and grandchildren have walked way out into the Wadden Sea at low tide far past the point where Eugene splashed down to see what we could discover. It is always an emotional experience for everyone. Somewhere out there in the shallow Wadden Sea, likely in a crevasse, the remains of my brother rest. My family will never forget these experiences of being together again at last.

Aerial photo at the location where S/Sgt. Eugene Darter splashed down in the Wadden Sea, illustrating his bailout from the smoking B-17, the strong wind that blew him out over the dike where seventeen-year-old Cornelius Ellen was walking, and finally the splashdown about one thousand feet from the dike.
(Image credit Google Earth)

The last two men who saw my brother, Doral Hupp (left) and Cornelius Ellen (right), at the site where S/Sgt. Eugene F. Darter landed on December 16, 1943. He hit the shallow water just to the left of Doral Hupp (note that the old windmill is about half a mile along the dike to the south or right of the men as shown in the previous photo). (Photo credit M. I. Darter)

Thank God that these two men survived the war and sixty more years. Doral had a great career, and he and Winnie raised four children over those years. We sadly lost Doral in 2007, and he was buried with full military honors in Arlington National Cemetery. I am so grateful for all the hours he spent with me discussing what happened on December 16, 1943.

Cornelius Ellen, Michael Darter, and two grandnephews Alex Bowles and Lorren Krantz out in Wadden Sea at low tide at the location where S/Sgt Eugene Darter landed at high tide (Note that the near-freezing-water depth at this location was up to Eugene's neck when he splashed down. Having lost lots of blood, he never had a chance and blacked out quickly and was "gone with the wind" out into the deeper channels of the sea.) (Photo credit M. I. Darter)

Cornelius Ellen and Michael Darter searching for Eugene in Wadden Sea at low tide (Photo credit M. I. Darter)

Cornelius Survival Also a Miracle

We were incredibly fortunate that Cornelius survived the war as he was grabbed by the Nazis the day he turned eighteen to be sent as a slave laborer into Germany to build aircraft or submarines or countless other war machines, and most likely, Cor would have died there. But he wasn't about to be sacrificed and leaped from the truck on a curve at night and escaped and hid out in an attic on Texel for nine months until the war ended. He then experienced the last battle of World War II on Texel during the former Georgian uprising, where hundreds of Georgian troops (former Russian POWs), to save their lives, had joined the German Army and realized they would be executed by Stalin upon returning home, so they hatched a plan to kill as many German troops as possible one early morning in April 1945. They did but not kill enough and did not capture the gun batteries, and thus, a battle broke out on Texel, where hundreds of Germans, Georgians, and local Dutch people were killed. The battle ended only when Canadian forces came ashore two weeks beyond VE day in the Netherlands. Cor witnessed this horrible bloodshed near his family home but survived. After the war, he was ordered by the Dutch government to fight in the Dutch East Indies in brutal jungle warfare, but he survived again. However, this even more horrible experience may have affected him for the rest of his life.

Famous Jutter

Cor was famous as a jutter or "beachcomber" on Texel, with his image on a bottle of Juttertje (a liquor). Beachcombing has been a significant part of life on Texel for centuries, and people in the past have literally lived off what the sea provided on the beaches. He spent most days walking and riding his old 1939 British Army bike on the beautiful Texel North Sea beach, picking up valuable cargos that had fallen from ships and had been washed ashore. Several tons of valuable cargo including French wine, cigarettes, lots of wood, iron, precious metals, rubber bales, furniture, bottles of all shapes and colors, and much more splash up on the Texel beaches throughout his lifetime. Cor told me once that virtually everything in his cottage had come from the sea. Flotsam is all around the entrance to his home in Oosterend village, which is very close to the location where he saw my brother splash down in the Wadden Sea.

Placing messages in a bottle and throwing them overboard from ships he traveled on was a favorite hobby of Cornelius. He had a trunk full of over five hundred letters written by people who discovered his bottles with a message from all over Europe and even North America. He often gave humorous presentations around Texel to tourists in hotels. I got to see him honored with the opening of the Beachcombers Museum one summer when I was visiting. He was sought out by many TV stations for interviews about his interesting life of beachcombing and sending messages in a bottle.

Cor Ellen, the most famous of Texel beachcombers, on the dike on Texel Island, collecting things from the sea with his 1939 English Army bike used to haul the "loot" (Photo credit C. J. Ellen)

Cor and I became good friends, and he was always happy to see me and my family every year. He also sent e-mails every few weeks or so. I will never forget the several "walks in the Wadden Sea" that we took together at low tide to the location where my brother Eugene splashed down. Cor even planted a large pole at the spot Eugene landed off the dike complete with radio earphones that stood for several years. Finding Cor Ellen and having him relay to me the last moments of my brother's life will always be an incredible miracle that helped bring closure to me and the Darter family. And I will never forget the times at the end of each visit that I followed Cor on my bike and he on his old bike halfway across the island as he made sure that I did not get lost. We always shook hands warmly and wished each other well till we met again next year.

We lost Cor on May 6, 2012, in a hospital in Amsterdam. Cor's ashes were taken by family and friends and scattered into the Wadden Sea, not far from where the young American airman he witnessed sixty-nine years previously splashed down and was "gone with the wind" as he often stated.

Hans Eelman of Texel attended the placing of Cor's ashes in the Wadden Sea on September 23, 2012, and wrote the following:

> *Yesterday we went with about 40 persons on the boat "Vrienschap" in the "Eierlandse Gat" near the lighthouse on the north of Texel. From there we went into the Wadden Sea and dropped the ashes of Cor beside the boat. He was the last person who saw your brother alive. Now they are together. It was a cold and windy day, the wind came from the east. Afterwards we dropped roses and took a drink. Cor Ellen was 85 years old.*

But I think the "king of beachcombers" is still out there roaming all along the beautiful Texel beaches and beyond, and I have no doubt that someday we will find on a nearby beach a message in a bottle from Cor Ellen.

Where Are Eugene's Remains?

Cor Ellen was helpless to prevent the American airman being pulled by half-moon parachute chords further out into the windy and stormy Wadden Sea until he disappeared into the fog and mist. Cor told me that Eugene collapsed in the water just prior to his being pulled out into the sea. Weakened Eugene quickly blacked out (hypothermia) as described by Lt. Harold Kious in Chapter 12. When the wind calmed and the chute settled down again into the sea, the outgoing tide flow would have carried his lifeless body closer to the deeper channels of the Wadden Sea. The flow and channels are illustrated in the Google Earth aerial photo in Chapter 12. Cor Ellen who lived his entire life on Wadden Sea shore believed that if he had not inflated his Mae West, this is likely where his remains, tethered to his chute, would have sunk to the bottom of the sea, perhaps in a deeper crevice, one to two miles from the Texel shore south from the village of Oost. Over time with the coming and going of the relentless tide and storms his remains would have been covered with sand.

In the unlikely event that Eugene inflated his Mae West vest, it would have carried his remains on the water, driven by wind and tide flows around the Wadden Sea. His remains could have potentially been pulled out with the strong tide current through the Marsdiep passageway between Den Helder and Texel ferry harbor into the North Sea.

Alternatively, the remains could have floated around the Wadden Sea pulled by wind and tide and washed up along the shoreline and became unidentified remains. During the war, when inhabitants of Texel (or other locations around the Wadden and North seas) discovered any human remains washed ashore, they were required to notify the authorities, and if military, were buried in the War Cemetery in Den Berg on Texel.

There is a special portion of the Texel cemetery (the War Cemetery) for burial of the war dead killed near Texel or washed up on the shore. The War Cemetery at Texel was the final resting place for many crews of Allied aircraft (at least twenty-three crashed during the war) and many remains of crews who washed up on the Texel shores from the North Sea and Wadden Sea. All Americans were disinterred after the war to Margraten. A careful examination of a detailed list of remains that washed ashore and were buried on Texel Island (including all Americans originally buried there) does not reveal any likely Unknowns after the December 16, 1943, date. A search of the Texel cemetery showed ten unknown military buried there, but none of the dates correspond to within months after the time when Darter landed in the Wadden Sea and Delbern and Neff in the North Sea. Cor Ellen watched each day for the airman's remains to wash ashore, but they never came.

There is a sign stating that all identified American military personnel were reinterred in the Netherlands American Military Cemetery at Margraten, Holland. This is also true for the many other cemeteries on other Frisian Islands, across the Wadden Sea on the mainland, and throughout north Netherlands. Thus, if Eugene's remains washed ashore somewhere around the Wadden Sea or perhaps even if they floated out into the North Sea and washed ashore, they would have been buried in a local cemetery and hopefully identified as an American soldier or airman and then finally disinterred at the end of the war at the Netherlands American Military Cemetery at Margraten. As described in Chapter 21, a thorough search of all X-files of Unknown burials at Margraten was made with no likely remains identified.

Our family prefers to simply think of Eugene as "gone with the wind" as Cor Ellen observed, and his remains are irrecoverable in the beautiful Wadden Sea not far from the Texel shore. He may be gone, but he will forever be in our minds and hearts.

CHAPTER 25

CLOSURE AT LAST

The only other photo of the *Lonesome Polecat II* crew was taken at Grand Island, Nebraska, in late October 1943 as they were outfitted with new flying clothes. From there, the crew flew off to war, taking the northern course in two new B-17s to Valley, Wales. They all look so young, brave, and full of life, yet close-ups of their faces (chapter 2) clearly show anxiety for their future. These young men of course had read the news reports of the horrific losses in the air war over Europe in 1943 but did not fully comprehend the dangers that faced them ahead and that their fate was pretty much sealed given the odds of survival of about 25 percent that they would survive their required twenty-five combat missions. But they had trained intensively for over a year for the fierce combat and the very adverse environment they would face at five miles up in the air over the skies of the Third Reich.

As this thoroughly researched true story shows, these ten young men certainly did their part to keep the world free, and we all owe them (and so many thousands like them) tremendous gratitude. Looking into their faces gives me great happiness that their experiences and sacrifices in World War II could be recorded especially for their many descendants and so many others to know of their sacrifices to keep us free.

Crew of the *Lonesome Polecat II* who were shot down on December 16, 1943.
(Back row standing from left to right: Royal L. (Pete) Jackson, Don P. Neff,
Frederick A. Delbern, and Junius E. (Ed) Woollen. Front row kneeling
from left to right: Loren E. Dodson, Frank V. Lee, Eugene F. Darter,
Robert T. McKeegan, Charles J. Schreiner, and Doral A. Hupp.
(Photo credit United States Army Air Corps)

The distinguished 95th BG high in the sky on a mission over Nazi Europe.
The Eighth Air Force lost more men over the skies of Europe than the entire
Marine Corps in WWII (Photo credit United States Army Air Corps)

At the luncheon in Hotel Opduin on Texel near the crash site of the B-17F honoring all those involved in this event, former crew member Doral Hupp told how he last saw Lt. Delbern just behind the cockpit of the *Polecat* and he appeared injured, holding his right arm and black-tinted face. Delbern also indicated to Doral that copilot Lt. Don Neff was fatally wounded in the cockpit. This occurred as the *Polecat* was approaching the Wadden Sea, descending toward Texel Island and the North Sea. Jack Betsema told how his father, Gerrit Betsema, had seen a B-17 fly low over his village of Oost, with one engine standing still and one smoking (the exact condition of the *Polecat* on that day). Michele Binsbergen told how when he was a young boy of twelve, he and his friend Cees Bonne, his brother Nick, and his father witnessed the terrifying low-flying *Polecat* roaring over the rooftops of his village of De Koog on the North Sea. He recalls how the German soldiers shot at the bomber as it quickly passed over and ran to the top of the large hilly dunes where they could see the North Sea, saying, "It went down," and indicating that no one came out of it.

Evidence shows that copilot Lt. Neff was fatally wounded by enemy aircraft fire west of Bremen and that Lt. Delbern was hit in his left arm and, after flying the severely damaged *Polecat* by himself from about twenty-nine miles west of Bremen to Texel Island, was finally killed when the aircraft hit the North Sea hard during the crash landing just off the beach. Lt. Delbern had struggled in the cockpit with just one arm to control the severely damaged *Polecat* all the way back to Texel and got all of the surviving crew out before trying to ditch. Fred and Don are certainly the heroes of the crew for saving their lives.

Later on that same day, on the other side of Texel on the long dike (Lancaster) just north of the village of Oost, the two men who saw my brother last stood and looked out on the Wadden Sea and recalled the events of that day nearly sixty years ago. Doral Hupp told how he had found Darter collapsed in a pool of blood on the aircraft floor, badly wounded and weakened with much loss of blood, and stopped his bleeding and got his parachute buckled on him upside down so he could pull the chord with his only good arm. Doral watched surprised as Eugene jumped right out of the aircraft with his chute opening as planned. Cornelius Ellen recalled how shocking it was to see an airman suddenly come through the clouds above his head, crying out desperately for help and splashing down out in the very cold Wadden Sea, where the wind was so great that it soon partially inflated his still-connected parachute and pulled him straight out and under in its wake, and without any boat, there was nothing he could do to save him. In Cornelius's words, he was "gone with the wind."

I was also on the dike, listening to their accounts, especially the words "gone with the wind," and was filled with the most incredible emotions and feelings, recalling how sixty years ago (as I have been told countless times by my mother and father), on his way to England, Eugene had come home on furlough to see his family, which now included his little baby brother, and was so thrilled that he flew me all over the neighborhood on a pillow. As he departed, he held me in his arms, and we all prayed on our knees for his safe return. And then he departed and vanished from our lives forever. No one could imagine then that more than sixty years would pass before we would be this close again.

I have come to know my brother Eugene very well and also pilot Fred Delbern from all of the things their crewmates shared with me as well Fred's wonderful wife Geri Marshal (Delbern). So when I touch their names on the wall at Cambridge cemetery, when I walk the old runway at the old Horham air base, and especially when I walk out into the Wadden Sea at low tide where Eugene died or the North Sea beach where Fred and Don died, I feel that for those few minutes each year, we are indeed together again and that, to me, they are no longer missing. Eugene is forever in my family's memory and hearts. Fred is forever in the heart of his beautiful sweetheart Geri and also the members of the Delbern family. And Don is still in the hearts of the Neff family. Had these three talented and dedicated young men's lives continued, there is no telling what they would have accomplished and the positive impact they would have had in the world. The sacrifice of these three brave men and those who flew with them will never be forgotten in the hearts of their families and the crew's families, as well as the 95th BG family. Never!

On a Boat in Wadden Sea

One Sunday in June, Gerrit Betsema invited me and my son Michael to sail with them and others on their boat in the Wadden Sea. We sailed near to the location where my brother had splashed down and held a memorial for the three still-missing crew members of the *Lonesome Polecat II*: Lt. Fred A. Delbern, Don P. Neff, and Eugene F. Darter. Those in attendance included Johan Graas (director of the Foundation for Aircraft Recovery

'40-'45), boat owner Gerrit Betsema, Michael Olsen-Darter (nephew to Eugene Darter), and myself (brother to Eugene Darter).

The first page of crewmate Lt. Ed Woollen's Red Cross diary includes this very touching memorial. It was written just weeks after Ed was badly wounded on board, ordered to bailout, was captured, put in solitary confinement, interrogated, and finally interred in a POW prison at Barth, Germany, in January 1944. One can hardly imagine his emotions and sadness at this moment of his life, but out of this sadness comes a most touching beautiful memorial with so much meaning for the families involved. This eulogy was read, and a bouquet of flowers was set upon the water. The event was recorded by TV North Holland and was aired the next day. "Gone with the wind" was my brother.

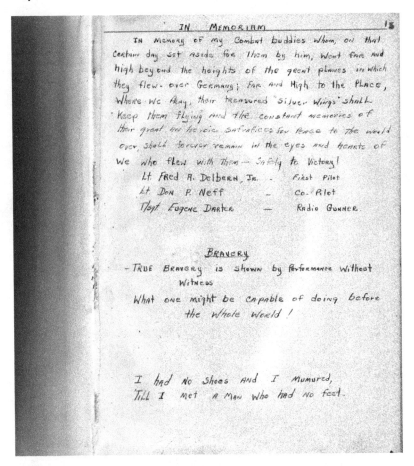

Memoriam (by Lt. Ed Woollen, 1944 as a POW)

In Memoriam (written by crew member Lt. Ed Woollen, 1944)[24]

In memory of my combat buddies whom,
on that certain day set aside for them by Him,
went far and high beyond the heights
of the great airplanes in which they flew over Germany;
far and high to the place, where we pray,
their treasured "Silver Wings" shall keep them flying
and the constant memories of their great and heroic sacrifices
for peace to the world over, shall forever remain in the eyes and
hearts of we who flew with them, safely to victory!
     Lt. Fred A. Delbern, Jr.—First Pilot (Right)
     Lt. Don P. Neff—Copilot (Center)
     T/Sgt. Eugene F. Darter—Radio, Gunner (Left)

Never Give Up the Search!

For those searching for their own loved ones, I encourage you to never give up. There is so much more information available and ways to find MIAs today, and this ability and resources will only increase in the future. The references at the end of this book show the addresses, phone numbers, e-mail addresses, and names of individuals and offices that helped me in this search. The American government has an unprecedented strong program to locate and identify MIAs throughout the world and to bring them home as promised. To these dedicated men and women of JPAC our family and many others thank with all our hearts.

As a fitting ending to this story, the following words are inscribed in the ceiling of the memorial chapel in the American Cemetery in Cambridge, England, where crew members of the *Lonesome Polecat II* are honored:

> *In proud and grateful memory of those men of the United States Air Force who from these friendly Isles flew their final flight and met their God. They knew not the hour, the day, nor the manner of their passing when far from home they were called to join that heroic band of airmen who had gone before.*
>
> *May they rest in peace.*

Dedicated to the brave crew of the *Lonesome Polecat II* (B-17F #42-30255) (Age listed at time of service)

Eugene F. Darter, California (thirty years old)
Frederick A. Delbern, Minnesota (twenty-four years old)
Loren E. Dodson, Illinois (twenty-six years old)
Doral A. Hupp, Ohio (twenty-three years old)
Royal L. (Pete) Jackson, Vermont (twenty-six years old)
Frank V. Lee, Tennessee (twenty-two years old)
Robert T. McKeegan, Pennsylvania (twenty-three years old)
Don P. Neff, Ohio (twenty-six years old)
Charles J. Schreiner, North Dakota (twenty-nine years old)
Junius E. (Ed) Woollen, North Carolina (twenty-nine years old)

A huge thank-you to you and thousands like you for your service that gave us our freedom!

LIST OF REFERENCES AND SOURCES OF INFORMATION

1. Individual deceased personnel file for Eugene F. Darter, S/Sgt, 39541802, Record Group 92: Records of the Office of the Quartermaster General, Washington National Records Center, Suitland, MD [a record of all investigations concerning E. F. Darter, MIA since December 16, 1943].
2. Interviews and personal communication with surviving crew members Doral A. Hupp (Virginia), Loren Dodson (Illinois), Charles Schreiner (California), and Pete Jackson (Arizona) from March 2000 to July 2007.
3. Missing Aircrew Report (MACR) 1558. National Archives at College Park, 8601 Adelphi Road, College Park, Maryland 20740-6001. [Note: This file can be requested for any aircraft that has crashed.]
4. Mission Report of the 95th BG for December 16, 1943. Many pages of material related to the mission of the 95th BG on that day, National Archives at College Park, 8601 Adelphi Road, College Park, MD 20740-6001.
5. Jeffrey L. Ethel, *Bomber Command*, ISBN 0-87938-920-6, published by Motorbooks International Publishers & Wholesalers, 1994.
6. Fritz Ulrich, *Rendezvous with Destiny*, Universal Publishers/uPUBLISH.com, USA, 2000.
7. Ian L. Hawkins, *B-17s over Berlin: Personal Stories from the 95th Bomb Group (H)*, Published with the cooperation of the 95th BG Bomb Group (H) Association (see 95th BG Web site), BRASSEY's, Washington and London, 1990.
8. *Contrails: The 95th Bombardment Group H*, US Army Air Forces, 1945.

9. *Contrails II: A Pictorial History of the* 95th *Bombardment Group (H)*, published by the 95th Bomb Group Association, 2003.
10. Robert Morgan, *The Man Who Flew the Memphis Belle*, New American Library, 2001.
11. Robert Cowley, ed., *No End Save Victory*, G. P. Putnam's Sons, NY, USA, 2001.
12. *Memphis Belle*, motion picture, Warner Bros., 1990.
13. Lloyd O. Krueger, *Come Fly with Me*, Published by to Excel, an imprint of iUniverse.com, Inc. 2000.
14. Paul M. Andrews, *Operational Record of the 95th Bomb Group (H)*, 1990.
15. Web site of German pilot Heinz Knoke, http://www.chez.com/franckruffino/Victoire_10.htm
16. Web site of the 95th BG Bomb Group Memorials Foundation (USA): www.95thbg.org
17. Web site of the 95th Bomb Group Heritage Association (UK): www.95thbg-horham.com
18. Stephen E. Ambrose, *The American Heritage New History of World War II*, September 1997.
19. World War II Honor Roll listing for Eugene F. Darter, American Battle Monuments Commission, Web pages, http://www.abmc.gov (this database includes the names of service persons, their units, state of entry, and date of death of those either buried in these cemeteries or listed as missing in action).
20. Personal communication with John A. Storey, pilot in 95th Bombardment Group, 2002.
21. Photos obtained from the old 95th BG aerodrome at Horham, England.
22. Personal communication with Mr. Arthur G. Watson, formerly S/Sgt in the 95th BG located at Horham, England, during the war 1943-1945.
23. Letter from Major Don B. Mohler, Headquarters, American Graves Registration Command, European Theater Area, APO 887, US Army, to Mr. W. van Poelje, dated May 14, 1946.
24. Personal communication with John Woollen (son of crew member Lt. Ed Woollen), 2001-2003.
25. Personal communication from Major Don B. Mohler, Headquarters, American Graves Registration Command, European Theater Area, US Army, to Mr. Francis M. Darter, dated December 17, 1943.

26. Personal communication with Harold Kious, 2001-04.
27. Personal communication with Cornelius Ellen, Texel, 2003-12.
28. Personal communication with P. K. Stark, Texel, 2001.
29. Diary of Mr. K. Kok for December 16, 1943, in possession of Mr. Jaap Bakker, Texel.
30. Personal communication with Mr. Johan Graas, president, North Holland Aircraft Recovery Association, Netherlands, 2000-2013.
31. Personal communication with Mr. Cees Bonnie, Texel, 2002-2004.
32. Personal communication with Mr. Michele Binsbergen, Texel, 2002-2009.
33. Geoffrey Perret, *Winged Victory: The Army Air Forces in World War II*, published by Random House, New York, NY, 1991.
34. Martin Bowman, *B-17 Flying Fortress Units of the Eight Air Force (Part 2)*, Osprey Combat Aircraft Series, Osprey Publishing Limited, 2002.
35. Text taken from the following Web site: http://www.angelfire.com/my/mighty8thlh/CHAPELUK.html
36. Personal communication (typed letter) from Charles Schreiner to Mrs. Fred A. Delbern, November 11, 1945.
37. German Claims on Western Front, December 16, 1943 (Film C. 2031/Il Anerk: Nr.10 and 11). B-17 down off Texel, near De Koog.
38. Adam Makos and Larry Alexander, *A Higher Call: An Incredible True Story of Combat and Chivalry in the War-Torn Skies of World War II*, Penguin Group Publisher, 2012.
39. John C. Walter, *My War*, published by AuthorHouse, 2004.
40. Robert M. Poole, *On Hallowed Ground: The Story of Arlington National Cemetery*, Bloomsbury Publishing USA, 2009.
41. Rob Morris with Ian Hawkins, *The Wild Blue Yonder and Beyond*, Potomac Press, Washington DC, 2012.
42. Fact Sheet, US Air Force, Eighth Air Force. Headquarters Eighth Air Force, Office of Public Affairs, Barksdale AFB, LA. 71110-2279. http://www.mightyeighth.org/Library/PDFs/8thAFfacts.pdf
43. Wikipedia, World War II Casualties by Branch of Service, http://en.wikipedia.org/wiki/World_War_II_casualties#Military_casualties_by_branch_of_service
44. *Summary Statistics*, Defense POW/Missing Personnel Office (DPMO), December 4, 2012.
45. Wikipedia: http://en.wikipedia.org/wiki/Joint_POW/MIA_Accounting_Command#cite_note-10

46. Michael I. Darter, *Fateful Flight of the Lonesome Polecat II*, iUniverse Publisher, 2004.
47. Personal communication with Hans Eelman, Texel, 2011-13.
48. Robert J. Mrazek, *To Kingdom Come*, NAL Caliber, Publisher, 2011, USA.
49. Personal communication with John Miller, Madison, WI, 2006.
50. Wikipedia: http://en.wikipedia.org/wiki/Missing_in_action
51. Wil S. Hylton, *Vanished: The Sixty-Year Search for the Missing Men of World War II, Riverhead Books Publisher*, New York City, NY, 2013.
52. Stuart Hadaway, *Missing Believed Killed*, Pan & Sword, Avation, 2012.
53. Fafnir Bearing Co., "23 tons of prodigious flying might", *Aviation*, July, 1942, p16. http://legendsintheirowntime.com/B17/Ads/B17_Av_4207_p016_150.png

INDEX

APPENDIX

SOME UP-TO-DATE SOURCES OF INFORMATION ON MIAS

A government agency that communicates with families of still missing MIAs is the Defense POW/Missing Personnel Office (DPMO), whose motto is "Keeping the Promise." They recently conducted a thorough search and investigation into all of the currently available records regarding my MIA brother that included many sources.

- Defense Prisoner of War, Missing Personnel Office (DPMO).

    DPMO sent me a detailed case summary report documenting everything they found related to my brother from these many documents from which I found new information. Anyone beginning a search for their MIA has a valuable resource in DPMO.

    Department of the Army
    US Army Human Resources Command
    Past Conflict Repatriations Branch
    1600 Spearhead Division Avenue
    Fort Knox, KY 40122
    Visit DPMO Web site at http://www.dtic.mil/dpmo
    or call 800-892-2490

- Individual deceased personnel file (IDPF)
  - o Records of the Office of the Quartermaster General, Washington National Records Center, Suitland, MD.

- Missing aircrew report (MACR) 1558.
  - o The missing aircrew reports of the US Army Air Forces, 1942-1947, National Archives Microfilm Publication M13380, Record Group 92

- Records of the Office of the Quartermaster General, National Archives, College Park, MD.
- World War II Honor Roll listing for any service person buried or MIA overseas.
  - o American Battle Monuments Commission (ABMC). http://www.abmc.gov/home.php

- Enlistment record for service person, Electronic Army Serial Number Merged File, ca. 1938-1946, World War II Army Enlistment Records, Record Group 64: Records of the National Archives and Records Administration, National Archives, College Park, MD. Searchable database accessible from this Web address: http://aad.archives.gov.aad
- Request for family information with **Freedom of Information** request. Request a copy of the Individual Deceased Personnel File (IDPF) X-files.
  > Army Human Resources Command's Freedom of Information Act Program.
  > Freedom of Information and Privacy Act Office, (502) 613-4203.

- JPAC: The Joint POW/MIA Accounting Command is a joint task force within the United States Department of Defense whose mission is to account for Americans who are listed as Prisoners Of War, or Missing In Action, from all past wars and conflicts. http://www.jpac.pacom.mil
- Information on personnel-related records might be maintained by the National Personnel Records Center. Make a written request for information to the National Personnel Records Center, Military Personnel Records, 1 Archives Drive, St. Louis, MO

63138. For more information on NPRC, visit their site at http://www.archives.gov/st-louis/.

- Army historical records which contain unit histories may be on file at the U.S. Army Heritage and Education Center, Attn: Patron Services Division, 950 Soldiers Drive, Carlisle, PA 17013-5021.
- Although unit histories do not normally include information about specific personnel, they will show the unit's activities and participation during the war. For more information on USAHEC, visit their site at http://www.carlisle.army.mil/ahec/.
- Official Army unit records prior to 1939 may also be found at the Military Reference Branch National Archives and Records Administration, 700 Pennsylvania Avenue, NW Washington, DC 20408-0001. Tel: 1-866-272-6272/ http://www.archives.gov/dc-metro/.
- From 1939 onward, including units that served in Southeast Asia: Modern Military Records National Archives and Records Administration, 8601 Adelphi Road College Park, MD 20740-6001. Tel: 301-837-3510/ http://www.archives.gov/dc-metro/college-park/.
- The New York Public Library may also contain Army unit records. For more information visit their site at http://www.nypl.org/.

ABOUT THE AUTHOR

Michael I. Darter is an emeritus professor of civil and environmental engineering at the University of Illinois at Urbana-Champaign. He received his PhD in civil engineering from the University of Texas at Austin and is an international expert in transportation engineering infrastructure. However, he often states that nothing he has accomplished in his profession has been as satisfying as discovering what happened to his only brother Eugene whom he met and bonded with as a baby.

He has mourned his loss for decades and many years ago pledged to find out what happened to him no matter what it took to bring closure to his family. Darter is equally thrilled that the discovery of what happened to all three of the MIA crewmembers who paid the ultimate sacrifice also brought heartwarming closure to the crews' families and especially to the former wife (now 95 years young) of pilot Fred Delbern who finally knows what happened to her beloved husband.

CPSIA information can be obtained
at www.ICGtesting.com
Printed in the USA
FSHW01n2308290718
51004FS